'*Grace-Filled Marriage* is a mus
couple. Accessible yet rich with :
and-all glimpse of the challenge
refreshing to read honest examp
I cried and at times I laughed out loud – demonstrating
and downs of what it means to commit your life to another person,
despite our personal differences and the challenges and situations life
throws at us all. The book weaves together the story of marriage, the
intertwining of lives, the importance of the support of community
and the recognition of a grace that comes only from God.'

Chine McDonald, writer, broadcaster and head of
public engagement at Christian Aid

'We will be the first to admit that, while marriage can be a source of
incredible joy, it can also be a source of the deepest pain. Marriage,
like life, isn't black and white. It's a complex mix of joys and challenges, growing and changing, wounding and forgiving, receiving
and sacrifice. For that reason, we are grateful for the humility and
wisdom of Steve and Claire Musters as they invite us into the practical challenges they've faced as a couple and share how God can bring
hope, healing and redemption as we take our eyes off ourselves and
turn our eyes to him.'

Jeff and Sarah Walton, authors

'With forthright honesty, Steve and Claire Musters share their own
personal challenges faced in marriage and, drawing from others'
experiences, they bring the practical application of grace to every situation. A wake-up call to not be passive and let your marriage drift,
but to grow in love through allowing God's grace to change you.'

David and Liz Holden, New Community Church,
SE London; leaders, New Ground family of churches,
part of Newfrontiers

'Who would you rather learn from when it comes to marriage: the couple sailing through blissfully without challenge, or the couple who have been stretched to the limit but have come through it stronger and more resilient as a result? *Grace-Filled Marriage* is testament that a marriage can experience disillusionment, disappointment, even infidelity, yet break through to growth and joy. Here are the hard-wrought principles Claire and Steve Musters have learned along their way.'

Sheridan Voysey, author

'Claire and Steve's story is a brutally honest insight into their marriage journey and how they've applied God's grace to all aspects of their relationship. With additional stories from other couples, this book explicitly illustrates not only the reality of the everyday challenges of married life but also the deep richness of this unique relationship that God has planned. The chapters on trust and forgiveness powerfully show how biblical truths can be applied as important foundations to help build a healthy and thriving marriage. The 'Over to you' sections provide helpful questions to kickstart discussions, which will enable couples to apply what they are learning in their own situations. We pray that this book will be a real encouragement for couples to press on towards a grace-filled marriage.'

Andy and Fiona Banes, Executive Directors of Time for Marriage

'Real, and in places raw and vulnerable, this book is an honest account of building a marriage through tough times. Claire and Steve don't pull their punches, but give us a rare glimpse into working through some of the challenges which, if we are honest, come to every marriage at one time or another. Grounded in Scripture, their insights offer us the precious gift of knowing we aren't alone in our struggles, and that our marriage itself can be a beautiful gift of God's grace.'

Katharine Hill, UK Director, Care for the Family

Grace-Filled Marriage

Strengthened and transformed through God's redemptive love

Claire and Steve Musters

Authentic

First published 2021 by Authentic Media Limited,
PO Box 6326, Bletchley, Milton Keynes, MK1 9GG.
authenticmedia.co.uk

British Library Cataloguing in Publication Data
A catalogue record for this book is available from the British Library.
ISBN: 978-1-78893-138-0
978-1-78893-139-7 (e-book)

Cover design by Vivian Hansen
Printed and bound by CPI Group (UK) Ltd, Croydon, CR0 4YY

Copyright Acknowledgements

We would both like to dedicate this book to our parents, as each couple modelled loving, long-lasting marriages to us despite huge challenges.

From Claire: My parents overcame many obstacles and differences to forge a deeply tender marriage. In its final years, Dad cared selflessly for all of Mum's physical needs – right up until the moment she died (which happened while we were in the middle of writing this book). I'm so grateful for their example of sacrificial love.

Contents

Foreword

It seems to me that there aren't enough real conversations within the church when it comes to relationships, whether that be about marriage, singleness, dating or divorce. Potentially, this comes from a fear of offending, or of getting into difficulties knowing that if we talk about strengthening marriage, it could upset those who have been through divorce or it would seem insensitive to those who are single and would rather not be. Equally, some would say that what goes on behind closed doors is something we shouldn't share or interfere with. Then there's the risk of vulnerability that we may be exposed to in our own marriages if we raise the subject. Yet learning to manage and thrive within your current relationship status should be a priority in Christian community.

For our younger generation within the church, there has often been an emphasis on what you shouldn't 'do' as a Christian in a relationship rather than teaching through the experience of others about healthy relationships, leading to healthy marriages (which by the way are not perfect ones!). This must include the good times and the times of challenge. Grace-filled teaching and sharing of experience can lead to healthy relationship choices in every area of our lives, therefore impacting us spiritually, emotionally, mentally and physically.

Many churches offer marriage preparation before a couple begins married life together, and then, all too often, there seems to be an assumption that if couples love each other, they will get on with it and just work it out. However, as this book illustrates, it's not that simple!

There are now many more courses available for couples who are married, and as the coordinator of UK National Marriage Week, I'm encouraged to hear stories of couples who choose to invest in their marriages. Yet there are still too many couples who believe that marriage courses are something you turn to when things go wrong rather than to enrich your marriage. Again, I would suggest that this is due to the lack of conversation around this subject, and as churches, I believe that we need to normalize discussion around relationships, which is in part why this book is so hugely welcome.

Social media perpetuates the notion that if you do have any problems in your marriage, small or large, there must be something wrong with you, since everyone else is apparently doing fine. Despite logically knowing that what is seen on social media can't be the constant reality of these marriages, the veneer presented in these posts reinforces an artificial world of perfection, and an expectation that we ought to be able to have a strong marriage. This pressure can be greater within the church because surely, as a Christian couple, we should be able to do marriage well since it's God's great idea? Once again, as couples and individuals, we are crying out for honest conversation in this area.

Marriage is an everyday symbol and manifestation of the relationship between Christ and his bride – the church. However, as the 'bride of Christ', we are acutely aware that we are not a perfect body of people, that we do indeed make mistakes and that our 'marriage to Jesus' is an ever changing, growing and learning relationship underpinned by the grace of God. As individuals, as the body, we seek his redemptive love, but do we ever stop to consider and actively seek it out for our marriages too?

In this grace-filled, hope-filled, honest, vulnerable book of wisdom, Claire and Steve challenge the perception that marriage problems should not be spoken about and, more than that, they highlight the call on us as couples to actively position our marriages within the redemptive love of God. *Grace-Filled Marriage* is pioneering something that is crucial for marriages and for the symbol of marriage within the church. Claire and Steve share their experiences, including their mistakes, the lows and the unfiltered truth, so that other couples can learn, grow and also experience a grace-filled marriage with God at the centre.

Not only have they shared their personal accounts, they've also invited a number of other Christian couples to contribute a part of their marriage story. This includes couples from across the globe, from a variety of church traditions and with a range of life experiences and challenges, such as mental and physical ill-health, infertility, cultural differences and one of the biggest challenges to all marriages: the subtle but dangerous journey of drifting apart and losing intentionality.

As executive director of the national charity Marriage Foundation, I'm acutely aware of the value of marriage to couples, children and society as a whole. Our research has given us a voice to champion marriage on a national level since it has demonstrated time and time again that marriage is the gold standard for couples who want to go the distance. And while we are realistic and recognize that not every marriage will work, the good news is that divorce rates have been falling since the peak in the 1980s and continue to do so. Marriage is still, by far, the most successful relationship choice for couples. So, what makes marriage stand apart? It's the intentional choice to commit to our partner, which begins on our wedding day and continues each and every day of our married life.

This book will take you on a journey as a couple, with frank and relatable, real examples and through offering you the chance to demonstrate your ongoing daily commitment to each other with short reflective questions at the end of each chapter. It will challenge you, help you to celebrate what is going well and encourage you to continually invite God's loving hand to direct you as you navigate married life together.

I'm a Christian and I've been married for more than 20 years and I'm very grateful to Claire and Steve for writing their story, for bringing fresh challenge to me in my own marriage and, since we are all learning, I'm convinced this book will do the same for you and your marriage, whether you feel it is in an exceptionally good place or quite the opposite. My prayer is that, as the imperfect bride of Christ, we will embrace his grace in every area of our lives – that within our communities we will invite him to redeem our marriages and to keep the relationship conversation going for this generation and the next and the next and the next. As Proverbs 1:5 says: 'Let the wise listen and add to their learning.'

Michaela Hyde, Executive Director, Marriage Foundation
Marriagefoundation.org.uk

Introduction

My grace is sufficient for you, for my power is made perfect in weakness.

2 Corinthians 12:9

Marriage is hard. Let's just get that out there. That statement will probably come as no surprise to you if you are married. Yet marriage is also an incredibly beautiful and powerful gift of grace from God. It is a unique relationship, one in which we come into the closest proximity possible with another human. We live with our partner every day, sleep in the same bed, share our deepest secrets, allow our bodies to entwine as we give them to each other in sexual intimacy. As those made in the image of God, we are made to love and be loved, and marriage is a beautiful outworking of that. It is a wonderful demonstration of the glory and grace of God. And yet. It is also a relationship that costs us dear and can cause us so much pain. We desperately need God's help, and his grace, in order to navigate this most precious of relationships well.

We have been married for nearly thirty years and know only too well both the intimacy and the loneliness, the joy and the pain, the running together and the running away from each other that, if we are honest, most marriages experience in different seasons of life. We have read many books on how to have a better marriage over the years. Some have been incredibly helpful, but what we missed was learning from marriages that weren't just models of perfection, but models of God's grace – his undeserved favour – in the messiness of real life.

We attended a marriage course led by a lovely older couple many years ago. However, when they admitted that they rarely argued and their one example of a 'painful period' was when one of them spoke in a tone that upset the other, we began to think: 'What hope have we got?'

Yet part of the beauty of marriage is that God brings imperfect people together in such a way as to reveal his love to the world – in sacrifice, in intimacy, in redemption and in partnership. Yes, it is messy, yet it can also be one of the most powerful visual demonstrations of God's grace, as we allow him to change us and mould us together – often using the very challenges and difficulties we face to do so.

In this book, our own story of building back a marriage after loneliness, betrayal and separation is also joined by several other stories of marriages where each partner has chosen to hold onto God's grace – and each other – in the midst of the specific challenges of their own relationships. Those challenges include infertility, physical and mental ill health, cultural differences, as well as dealing with mistakes and broken areas of their lives.

We are so grateful to every contributor for their vulnerability, honesty and wisdom. Sometimes it is refreshing to hear about the failings, the doubts, the wrestling . . . because it helps us to face our own with courage. We feel we are not alone – and that is *so* important. That is what we hope will happen when you begin to read this book: that those of you who need to know you are not alone will hear that message – as well as one of hope.

Of course, you may feel you have a great marriage already, which is fantastic. Might we gently suggest that it is always good to have a reminder to continue working at and enjoying the lifelong relationship God has blessed you with. But there may be moments of regret that punctuate your marriage, which could still be having an impact on it today. Our prayer is that, through our own honesty about our big mistakes and the struggles we have faced at different times in our journey, you will remember the faithfulness of God and how his hand of grace is on each of our lives – and our marriages too. He is 'making everything new' (Rev. 21:5), and that includes our closest relationships. We have been learning so much about how he uses our marriages as a means of purifying, changing and moulding us, even as we have been writing. It has been painful at times, to have such a close spotlight on our own relationship. While looking back with such thankfulness at the redeeming work God has done, we also recognize the work that *still* needs to be done on our characters as well as the way we interact with one another.

Marriage and the gospel

Steve: The reason we should hold marriage in such high regard is because it truly is a wonderful picture of Jesus' relationship with his church: how he loves us with all our imperfections and hang-ups, all our insecurities and quirks, and transforms us into whole people that radiate that same grace to each other. Only in knowing the gospel can we truly understand marriage. It motivates us to be gracious and to extend forgiveness – even when the other person doesn't deserve it – because we know what Christ has done for us. We can also come to understand that we don't need to look to the other to 'complete' us, to provide that love, acceptance and significance that we all long for (I know Claire looked for this in many places when she didn't find it in me). When we truly understand that we are accepted, chosen and fully loved by God we can then learn to love our partner from a place of grace and mercy – and overflow, because as we allow the Spirit to work more deeply and more fully in us, his love overflows to those around us.

When we understand that marriage can be a means by which we come to understand God better, we can begin to view it very differently. Historically, marriage has simply been seen as the bedrock of society – an institution that is fundamental to the stability and welfare of our children and our future. While there is truth in that, it is only a tiny part of the story. More recently, this understanding of marriage has changed to a far more individualistic one: a view that marriage exists for me. It is simply an agreement between two people for mutual benefit – sexual, financial or emotional. The natural outcome of that view is that when that benefit to me ceases, then the marriage has no worth. In other words, with this view, marriage is only as valuable as what I get out of it.

Yet as we begin to understand God's bigger picture of marriage better, we see that right from the beginning marriage was all about mission. From Genesis 2 we see two people co-labouring together to demonstrate God's love, order and beauty to the world. It is a beautiful image of partnership and friendship. As Ecclesiastes 4:9–10 says: 'Two are better than one, because they have a good return for their labour: If either of them falls down, one can help the other up.'

As Scripture unfolds, we see how marriage becomes this picture of God's love for his people. The Song of Solomon graphically describes God's passionate, jealous, pursuing love: 'Place me like a seal over your heart, like a seal on your arm; for love is as strong as death, its jealousy as unyielding as the grave. It burns like blazing fire, like a mighty flame. Many waters cannot quench love; rivers cannot sweep it away' (Song 8:6–7). This pursuing, passionate love was ultimately demonstrated in Jesus' sacrificial love toward his bride, the church. And we know that this relentless love will culminate in a wedding as Christ returns for his bride (Rev. 19:7). Scripture is bookended with weddings. Our own marriages, therefore, become sermons about God's love towards his creation – about Jesus' love for his church. Each marriage is a picture of sacrifice – of giving ourselves to another – but ultimately a picture of grace and redemption through Christ. No longer is marriage just for our fulfilment, comfort and convenience, but rather a way in which God is revealed. The gospel really is the beating heart of marriage. When we see it in those terms, we can perhaps understand why marriage has been so under attack from the very beginning.

We will never forget walking down a street in south London, where we noticed a multitude of small flags that had been hooked up on ropes hanging between lamp-posts. The friends we were visiting explained that each flag represented a Christian marriage, and that it was local witches who had put up the flags – they were actively seeking ways to destroy them. Our marriages are precious, and vital for the furthering of the gospel – and our enemy knows that!

We all need grace

Claire: Our marriage rapidly fell apart towards the end of its first decade, and the very night I had walked out on Steve a small group of our closest friends got together to pray for us.

One of the guys said something that annoyed me when he shared it with me a little later, as my sinful heart found it condescending. However, I've since recognized that it spoke of an attitude of gratitude and a mind that knew we are all capable of deeply wronging one another: 'There but for the grace of God go I.' He knew that it could have been any one of our marriages, and was grateful for the grace that God had shown him in his own. He then prayed for that same grace to cover ours.

We have seen that prayer answered so deeply in our own lives. And all that we say within the pages of this book is covered by God's grace. We can't create a 'successful' marriage in our own strength, but his perfect righteousness covers us. He upholds us, because he has already defeated every power and principality, and every temptation, that comes against us on the cross . . .

When I walked down the aisle as a 20-year-old romantic, I was completely naive and uninformed about what marriage truly was. Yes, I took my vows seriously, and had spent a long time pondering them as I worked through whether to include the traditional 'submit' part or not. But I don't think the enormity of what I was doing actually hit me. Marriage can be such a beautiful thing, but it can also be a battle – against the difficulties of life, against the lies and disappointment that can plague us so soon after the celebrations.

'For better or for worse' really sums up what we each face in our marriages: incredible highs but also 'I can't believe this is happening to us' lows. Somehow, as Christians, we can have the tendency to assume that with God in our marriage and with the right tools we can have the perfect marriage. And yet we forget we are fallen beings that, yes, are being perfected, but that perfection won't arrive until heaven and so we are navigating life as two 'works in progress'. This means there will be a lot of mess along the way! And, as we've come to learn, suffering is often the way that God shapes and moulds us, so it is a unique marriage indeed that doesn't include suffering of some form or other. Thank God that he is powerful enough to be glorified even through our imperfect marriages.

The vows at any wedding I attend now make me really emotional, probably because I know what they truly mean and what we have lived through in order to still be standing. I don't know if we would have listened if an older couple had tried to tell us about all this before we got married, but I do think it would be a good idea for us all to be more honest about the fact that marriage can be a struggle as well as a thing of utter beauty. Because none of us is capable of keeping those vows in our own strength – but, by the grace of God, we can.

The good news is that God is totally and utterly committed to us as individuals – and as couples. Marriage was his idea, so he doesn't leave us stranded in it, even if it feels like that sometimes! He gives us the strength to fight when we need to.

As you start to read this book, know that God's grace covers you – and each other. We have included some questions for you to ponder together at the end of most chapters, so that you can begin to apply the suggestions made in your own marriage. There will be times when you each fall short. Remember you are two imperfect people joined together through God's love. We all need God's grace – let's extend it to one another too.

Grace Kills Complacency

I will . . . transform the Valley of Trouble into a gateway of hope.
Hosea 2:15, NLT

Steve: I slumped on the mat in our entrance hall. The prover-bial rug had truly been pulled out from under my feet. As I sat there, though, an unwelcome thought lodged in my head: how complacent must I have been not to have seen this coming?

Complacency is an interesting word. As I found out, though, it is also one of the most destructive. Its Latin root simply means 'very pleased', and who doesn't want to be very pleased? The trouble is, in my marriage I had confused complacency with contentment – two very different things that are actually poles apart.

I think the simplest way I can differentiate between the two is by saying complacency is an uncritical view of life – it ignores deficiencies, it doesn't seek answers and, as such, gives a false sense of security that things are really OK when they aren't. Contentment is being well aware of any deficiencies, yet refusing to lose hope. Contentment proactively seeks to improve the situation without losing any sense of inner peace. Complacency is passive. Contentment is very active.[1] Moving from complacency towards contentment has certainly been a journey of discovery I have had to go on, and at times that journey has been incredibly painful.

Early struggles

I knew there were deficiencies in our marriage. Claire and I had known each other when we were active members of our church youth group. We had been great friends, but nothing more, until I returned from a trip to Africa and we decided that we were definitely more than good friends! We married when Claire finished her second year of university, which meant we were very young and very naive.

Shortly before we married, I had managed to get a job in a London recording studio and began investing myself in that industry, while Claire completed her degree course. As those early years progressed, we managed the best we could but, in reality, we were being forced to live almost separate lives due to my work commitments.

While our marriage was struggling, my career was flying. I was incredibly fortunate to work with artists at the top of their game, but my creativity also found an outlet in helping to shape new artists with freshly signed recording contracts as they sought to find their own voice and sound. I also had some wonderful opportunities to talk about my faith with people that few others ever get access to. In fact, looking back, possibly the thing I miss most about that job are those 3 a.m. conversations about faith, life and purpose. It was deeply rewarding, yet at the same time physically and emotionally exhausting.

In an industry that rarely sleeps, at night anyway, my hours, coupled with too many weekends apart, were not conducive

> It is interesting how quickly you can become comfortable with dysfunction.

to any relationship. Factor in a feeling that there wasn't anything we could do about it, and we simply settled into a dysfunctional state. Coping, most of the time, yet not flourishing. Surviving, just, but never thriving. It is interesting how quickly you can become comfortable with dysfunction.

The warning signs were clearly there. Claire would store up her frustration as long as she could, then about once a year it would all come out – unfiltered, loud and clear. But I knew things would calm down eventually and life would go back to normal – wouldn't it?

Ignoring the signs

When Claire first went to college in London I would drive up from Bath every weekend to see her. My mode of transport was an original Mini Cooper with a loud exhaust and low rally-style gearing. It was beautiful to behold, in British racing green, but it was not made for motorway cruising! Needless to say, the journey was draining. The noise, coupled with the sheer boredom of the M4 motorway, would eventually get to me and my eyelids would become heavier and heavier. I should have read the signs – literally flashing up on the gantries – 'Don't drive tired'. I should have stopped for a coffee; that would have been the sensible thing to do. But no, I kept going, and kept ignoring the signs, physically and literally, until (far more often than I care to let on) the rumble strips at the edge of the road would sharply awaken me as the car started to drift off the road.

Being lulled into a false sense of security on the road can be devastating, but so too can complacency in marriage. Claire had been my 'rumble strip' for a while, yet real change was required – not some temporary shake-up only to return to an apathetic stupor again.

My reluctance to recognize the gravity of our situation, or to try to do anything about it, was rooted in two places. Firstly, I wasn't sure *what* I could do about it. It was easier to keep my head down and keep going, particularly as I wasn't faced with the home situation all the time; I was shut away in the studio and literally 'lost in music'. Why is it that when we don't know what to do, we do nothing? Either that, or ignore reality by burying ourselves in stuff that distracts (and that is so often our work). Why don't we actually ask for advice from trusted friends instead? For me, not only did I not know what to do, but also I didn't really want to own up to the fact that we had a problem in the first place – a topic that Claire covers brilliantly in her book *Taking Off the Mask*.[2]

Complacency and pride are all too common partners. I know I can have the tendency to paper over the cracks, to put that brave face on and play the part. I'd downplay Claire's sense of desperation by saying, 'What if I was in the armed forces or a doctor? It would be the same.' Sadly, while I tried hard to ignore the situation, burying my head in the sand saying, 'What can I do anyway?' Claire's desperation and resentment grew. The phrase I heard from her over and over was, 'Things have to change!'

The painful wake-up call

That 'change' happened in one deeply painful moment early into a new year. Claire told me she was leaving, as she could not see a way forward for us any longer. Even more painfully, she was leaving with the husband of another couple in the church we attended.

So many things spiralled around in my head at that moment –
a heady mixture of denial, fear and anger. But what I remember
most is simply deep, heart-wrenching, gut-sickening sorrow at
my own complacency. I collapsed on that hallway mat.

Wake-up calls come in different shapes and sizes – I guess
you could class this as a big one! Over the next few days, as
I tried to come to terms with how on earth we had got to
this point, I felt a sense of complete helplessness and yet, deep
down, I had a desire to fight. To fight against despair. To fight
against hopelessness. To fight for my marriage.

The emptiness of the house, though, was a constant reminder
of the apparent hopelessness of the situation. It's funny what
you think about during periods of loss. I remember looking
around the bedroom that we were planning on decorating, and
thinking: 'What is the point now? There is no one to share it
with.' Like many people who have faced traumatic experiences,
I would wake up every morning with a feeling that it was all a
bad dream and then experience the horrible wave of realization
that it wasn't.

Still, deep down, there was an unquenchable desire to fight.
I cried out to God saying that I refused to be just another sad
statistic, another broken marriage, another product of busy
lives going off the tracks. One particular day, as I was praying/
crying/moping, I distinctly felt God give me a choice. I have
never heard the audible voice of God, but this was so close
to that in its clarity. I felt God say: 'What do you want? Do
you want out or do you want to fight for this marriage?' I felt
a swell of faith come into my heart, and I replied: 'I meant
the vows I made to Claire – I want to fight.' A wave of peace
came over me, and I slept well that night. Unbeknown to me
at the time, that conversation with God happened at the very

moment God convicted the guy who Claire had left with and prompted him to go back to his wife.

Learning from Hosea

I knew God was for marriage and I knew he was for *our* marriage. It is often said that it's when you are in the midst of the storm that you can feel God the closest. That is certainly my experience. Although all my securities – things I had grown so comfortable and complacent about – seemed to be shaken to dust, God was ever solid and ever present. Despite all the mistakes we had made, I somehow had faith that he could turn the situation around. He is, after all, the God who once took his disciples right through a storm on a lake in a small fishing boat – not to give them a scare and see how they coped, but to reveal more of who *he was* (Mark 4:35–41). When all around is in turmoil and threatening to pull you under, he is the one who is totally in control and, just as importantly, with you right there in the midst of the chaos and confusion.

In my helplessness, all I could do was call on him to change people's hearts and turn things around. I could sense that God was doing just that. Claire called me straight after the guy she had been with left, to let me know and to tell me she was going to live with her parents for a while. The fight was on!

I quickly discovered that the fight happens on many levels. Internally I had to fight against despair, when the only messages and signals I got back from Claire were: 'It is no use I have made up my mind, I can't go back to what we were.'

I had to fight against my own sense of self-righteousness, owning up to how much of a part I had played in the breaking down of our marriage, but also refusing to hold on to resentment and offence.

The story of Hosea in the Old Testament was so helpful in this area. In fact, I found and read Claire's copy of Francine Rivers' novel *Redeeming Love*, which is based on this book of the Bible. I had thought Francine Rivers' books were read by middle-aged ladies as a Christian alternative to Mills & Boon. How wrong I was! Who knew that her book would fundamentally challenge my sense of self-righteousness and cultivate grace in my heart, as I saw God's love radically demonstrated through Hosea's actions.

God gave the prophet Hosea an unbearably tough instruction. He was asked to marry Gomer, an unfaithful woman, to demonstrate God's unrelenting love and faithfulness towards the people of Israel despite their continuing unfaithfulness. Hosea literally acted out a prophetic picture of God's grace with his marriage. As his story unfolded, Gomer turned to other men – reflecting how Israel had turned from God to worship foreign idols and broken their covenant relationship. Time and time again God told Hosea to keep loving, to keep going back to Gomer and to keep pursuing her. Time and time again he did.

The story of Hosea spoke to me on many levels. Firstly, it put a little perspective on what I was going through. My situation was nowhere near what Hosea faced, but through this powerful illustration God gave me a way forward. I knew I was called to pursue Claire because that is what God models to us throughout Scripture – from going to great lengths to be with his people through the old covenant and its sacrificial system, to wooing Israel over and over again when they kept on rebelling against

> I knew I was called to pursue Claire because that is what God models to us throughout Scripture.

him. As we read through the books of the prophets we see both the pain of unfaithfulness (and therefore how God understands our pain) and the relentless love that he continued to extend. Of course, this demonstration of pursuing love was ultimately demonstrated in God sending Jesus Christ.

The call for husbands to love their wives as Christ loved the church (Eph. 5:23) is all too often watered down to simply mean putting your wife's interests before your own. Yet when we really look at how Christ loved the church we see it is so much more than that. In Jesus, God shows us what it really means to pursue someone you love. Jesus left the comfort and glorious splendour of heaven to enter the mess of our lives. Not because we showed any signs of promise but because, as Romans 5:8 says, he died for us 'while we were still sinners'. Even before we showed any hint of repentance, or even remorse, Jesus pursued us. He came for his bride, his church, to buy her back with his own blood; to redeem and purify her. One day he will return to bring her home.

It seems so unreasonable, but isn't that exactly what grace is all about? It is unreasonable because by very definition it is unearned, undeserved, unmerited and, dare I say, seemingly unjust.

So often we wait for others to show signs of commitment before we will commit. We will look more at trust in Chapter 3, but how often do we use the phrase 'trust must be earned'? Too often we give love only if we feel there is a chance of it being reciprocated. We forgive if there is sufficient evidence of regret demonstrated in an 'appropriate' way. Yet what God models to us is quite the opposite: he loves before we love, he commits even when we continue to break our commitment to him. He is steadfast in our fickleness and remains faithful in our unfaithfulness. He pursues those who simply don't deserve it. People like you and me.

I knew God was calling me to demonstrate that same relentless, unwavering love towards Claire. He had given me that model in Jesus Christ – now I needed his power to do it. Because what we also learn from Christ's example is that pursuing grace is never cheap. As 1 Peter 1:18–19 says: 'For you know that it was not with perishable things such as silver or gold that you were redeemed from the empty way of life handed down to you from your forefathers, but with the precious blood of Christ, a lamb without blemish or defect.'

It cost Jesus everything. He gave up his life for us and calls us to lay down our lives for each other (John 15:13). That means giving up the right to get even, to sulk, to make the other person suffer – or even to make sure they have really repented first. This love is risky – it has no guarantees other than one from Jesus: 'whoever loses their life for me will find it' (Matt. 16:25).

Persevering on the journey

I really had no idea where to start on this journey to love Claire unconditionally and refuse to give in to bitterness, rejection and self-centredness. Yet I began to feel the Holy Spirit helping me and directing me. My love was rejected many times, and for a long while there seemed to be no change, no chink in the protective armour that Claire had put up or any sign of breakthrough. I remember once travelling miles to find her favourite flowers to place on her desk. Although she was still living away at that time, she continued to work from her office at home. I could tell the response I got was more annoyance than affection, and yet I continued to be upheld and motivated by the Holy Spirit. I knew that the one who had pursued me, who had come from heaven to earth to pay the ultimate price for me, was also enabling me to persevere in hope and in grace.

Grace should never stop with us. As Jesus said: 'Freely you have received; freely give' (Matt. 10:8). As I continued to extend grace, the hard defences Claire had built up began to soften; in addition, the complacency that had built up in my heart couldn't get a look in either.

I'd like to be able to say that after so nearly losing my marriage I have learned my lesson, and apathy and complacency no longer get a look in. However, that's simply not the truth – and you probably wouldn't have believed me anyway!

I soon learned how quickly complacency tries to creep back in. I knew that my long hours in the studio were partly down to the fact that I throw myself into everything I do. I get totally focused and passionate about every last detail. I have now left that particular industry and lead a church. Again, this is the incredible grace of God . . . and yet sometimes I see the same traits creeping back in. This naturally sets off alarm bells in Claire, and old resentment, long since processed and dealt with, can try to resurrect itself. I still have to remind myself that my primary roles are as a husband and father, and that by God's grace I am called to pursue Claire with the same focus and attention to detail that I tend to pour into my job. The bottom line is that I am called to truly cherish my bride and make her *feel* cherished – and to do that complacency has to go on being killed.

Grace Covers Me

While he was still a long way off, his father saw him and was filled with compassion for him; he ran to his son, threw his arms round him and kissed him.

Luke 15:20

Claire: I am certainly not proud of what happened in our marriage, and the part that I played in its temporary breakdown. I know I was a very broken, devastated person when I acted the way I did, choosing to trust in another man rather than my husband; choosing to seek my own answers rather than trusting in God.

That said, I feel I need to acknowledge the fact that part of my frustration was because I felt I *had* kept surrendering our marriage to God. I *had* been crying out to him, over and over again. I know there will be those reading who are in really difficult situations (much worse than mine ever was) and you are tired of what feels like simply clinging on. Please know that you are not alone.

Looking for validation

Deep down, my issue was insecurity. I had such low self-worth that I looked for validation *everywhere*. The fact that my husband was not around, due to his working hugely long hours in a recording studio, may not have floored me in the way that it did had I been secure in my identity in God. After all, many marriages survive similar conditions (doctors, pilots, those working away for set periods for example). I know that it isn't ideal to be apart for too long, as it makes it hard to prioritize the relationship, but that doesn't mean such set-ups are an automatic recipe for divorce.

Sadly, for me, validation from God didn't seem to be enough. I know that sounds shocking to say, but I've realized now, looking back, that God wasn't my all-sufficiency in the way that he should be. He kept reminding me of his love through scriptures such as Jeremiah 31:3: 'I have loved you with an everlasting love; I have drawn you with unfailing kindness,' but it just wasn't tangible enough for me. While both Steve and I fell very short in our supporting roles in our marriage, I *should* have been able to find everything I needed in God, as 2 Peter 1:3 reminds us: 'His divine power has given us everything we need for a godly life through our knowledge of him who called us by his own glory and goodness.' But, as I explained in my book *Taking Off the Mask*,[1] we humans have a track record of looking to temporary, physical fulfilment, when much deeper, spiritual fulfilment is on offer. The latter seems too difficult, too 'out there' and, crucially, often involves waiting. We would much rather grab hold of what is right in front of us, even though we come to discover that it doesn't bring lasting happiness – and often can be very detrimental to our lives.

Just think of the Israelites: after God had rescued them in such an incredible way, and then provided manna in the desert, he called Moses up the mountain to receive the Ten Commandments. While he was gone, the Israelites got fed up of waiting and began to question who Moses even was. God said to him: 'Go down, because your people, whom you brought up out of Egypt, have become corrupt. They have been quick to turn away from what I commanded them and have made themselves an idol cast in the shape of a calf. They have bowed down to it and sacrificed to it and have said, "These are your gods, Israel, who brought you up out of Egypt"' (Exod. 32:7–8). While we may be quick to judge them, I know I can recognize the temptation to try and 'fix' things for myself through the physical rather than pressing in to God for more.

> God often does his deepest work in the waiting times.

I've learned more recently that God often does his deepest work in the waiting times. But we are impatient people, wanting the instant gratification that our culture says is our 'right'.

I've also come to understand that I liked to abdicate responsibility for certain vital things, like my spiritual wellbeing and my sense of contentment (see Chapter 8 for more on this). I had looked to Steve to fulfil me, lead me and make me feel good about myself. When I had cried out to God, he had told me that he wanted to be my husband and to teach me to rely on him for everything. Having felt that message resonate in my heart, he also led me to read Isaiah 54:5:

> For your Maker is your husband –
> the LORD Almighty is his name –
> the Holy One of Israel is your Redeemer;
> he is called the God of all the earth.

Sadly, I couldn't accept what God was offering me at that time. He went on to show me the subsequent verse too, which seemed to really describe how I was feeling:

'The LORD will call you back
   as if you were a wife deserted and distressed in spirit –
a wife who married young,
   only to be rejected,' says your God.

I *had* married young, and I *did* feel rejected and deserted. But I was angry that God was showing me he understood. Instead of turning towards him, I began to rebel, allowing my behaviour to spiral and using my hurt as an excuse. I even wrote in my journal after Steve and I had broken up that I know God had spoken to me about being my everything, and I had desperately wanted it, but I was confused and hurt because I had never experienced it. I felt I had never been passionate about my relationship with God, and *so* wanted to. And so I realized I had felt let down by that too. It was one of the things I had to wrestle with him about. But I can now see that if I had pursued a deepening relationship and had allowed him to teach me, then it would have made me, and my marriage to Steve, much healthier.

Heart 'surgery'

I was still serving others, still worshipping God – I just had a very divided, broken heart, and no amount of well-meaning sticking-plasters would hold it together. I could say all the right things, do all the right 'Christian' things, but deep down I was desolate. Every time Steve's recording session went on later than he thought it would (which was pretty much every day), my heart stung with

> I could say all the right things, do all the right 'Christian' things, but deep down I was desolate.

rejection. What I needed was heart 'surgery'. And, while I never intended to cause Steve, our friends, family, God and myself, so much agony, taking a stand to say enough is enough actually kickstarted something in both of us that desperately needed to happen.

It didn't start straightaway (for me at least). Because, in all honesty, I was a bit of a coward; as I said in *Taking Off the Mask*, I wore a mask of respectability, hiding behind what I did (and trying to find worth in it). But I also couldn't bear to be alone. I didn't take action, however, until I met a man who became someone I bared my soul to, someone who seemed to recognize and understand my pain. When he asked me to leave with him, I did. If I'm honest, I'm not sure whether I would have actually left Steve if it had meant being on my own. But that's exactly how I ended up, when that man decided he could no longer ignore God's insistent message that he needed to go home and work on his marriage in a way he never had before. At the time, I was totally devastated. I had pinned all my hopes for my future on him. Looking back, I am exceedingly grateful for God's grace over that situation – it could have been a whole lot messier if that relationship had gone on for longer, but it was over within a few weeks. Clearly, I was left forlorn, hopeless and in a lot of pain but, significantly, the first person I rang to tell what had happened was . . . Steve.

Hindsight is a wonderful thing. It is obvious now that for too long Steve and I had kept silent. For too long I had hidden behind romantic notions of what married life *should* be like. It was time for God to tenderly teach us the reality of living day-by-day with him. God stripped back all the lies and tended to the wounds, all the while affirming who we were. For me, having him speak loving, kind words after I had made such a mess of things spoke volumes to my devastated heart. Over this whole period, as I was left alone, and then back at my parents' house, I tangibly felt God running towards me, as he did to the prodigal son (see Luke 15:20). To have got things so wrong and yet still have his steadfast love being poured out over me daily really was my undoing. To begin with, I wanted nothing more than to sit at his feet and let him love me.

> God stripped back all the lies and tended to the wounds, all the while affirming who we were.

I need to acknowledge, however, that it took me a long time to recognize the pain I had inflicted – because I was completely enveloped in my own. I lapped up all the affirmation that God was pouring out over me, because that was what my love-starved heart was crying out for. And yet, ultimately, it took me much longer to realize how ridiculous my requests to God had been during those few weeks when I'd left Steve and was living at a friend's house alongside the other man. I spent time worshipping God, literally begging him to bless the action I'd taken – and asking him why I couldn't remain in close relationship with him while I continued on the course of action I had taken.

I think I equated Steve with such hurt, that I was at this point still blind to what I had done to him but, even more so, to God. I have always found what David says in Psalm 51 a little perplexing. It is the psalm that he wrote after Nathan the prophet confronted him about his adultery with Bathsheba. He had allowed his boredom to cause him to linger too long on the body of another man's wife – and then abused his position to get what he wanted, even going so far as to set up Bathsheba's husband Uriah's death! And then, having swept everything under the proverbial carpet, he had married Bathsheba and presumably thought that was that. Until Nathan came along and challenged him on his sin (see 2 Sam. 12:1–13). At that point, David had full realization of what he had done.

While God used David's psalm of repentance to gently begin working on my heart, I have to say there was always one line I found difficult (and still do to a certain extent): 'Against you, you only, have I sinned and done what is evil in your sight' (v.4). My response is to immediately think of all those who were simply pawns in his power game – Bathsheba, Uriah and Joab – and yet that misses the point. I was trying to fulfil my deep desire for love and security myself, through another human, and still keep hold of my close relationship with God. And yet through my sinful actions I was causing a separation from God that was completely of my own making. Ultimately, our sin is about missing the mark – God's mark. I had to learn to recognize that and repent of my actions, as they had caused a deep wedge between me and God; the decisions I had made had pained God and inevitably changed our relationship. As he describes the parental loving care he had shown towards Israel in Hosea, it also reveals the pain he must have felt when they turned their backs on him as, ultimately, I had unwittingly done. It wasn't until I had children of my own and they made decisions that hurt me directly that I truly understood this:

> When Israel was a child, I loved him,
> 　and out of Egypt I called my son.
> But the more they were called,
> 　the more they went away from me.
> They sacrificed to the Baals
> 　and they burned incense to images.
> It was I who taught Ephraim to walk,
> 　taking them by the arms;

but they did not realise
  it was I who healed them.
I led them with cords of human kindness,
  with ties of love.
To them I was like one who lifts
  a little child to the cheek,
and I bent down to feed them.

Hosea 11:1–4

Facing fear and rejection

There were a lot of other difficult realities that I had to face. After the other man had left me to go back to his wife and Steve had picked me up, packed my belongings up and driven me to my parents (where I was to stay for a good few months), I had to face the fact that I may have lost everything I had pinned my life on before (home, church, work, friends). That was when I came face to face with my deepest fear: being alone.

Another thing I struggled with in those first months, and even when we first got back together, was that I knew Steve was 'all in' – he was ready to work on our marriage. But for me, it felt like too much too soon. I was feeling hurt and rejected, and wasn't sure I could step back towards someone who, while I knew he loved me totally and unconditionally, had caused a lot of pain over the years. I needed to hear God's tender voice and allow his healing to come before I could even consider it. I was obviously also working through an enormous sense of rejection from the person who I had recently fallen in love with. He had made me feel special and loved, but at this point, I felt carelessly tossed aside, and also as if I was at the start of a huge uphill struggle. I needed time to hide away, to process all of that without Steve having to see it (although he did tenderly care for me during the times when it cropped up after we were back together).

There were moments in that period when my heart kept going astray; rather than continually focusing on the acceptance and healing God was offering without measure, I found myself pinning my hopes on the other man, who had told me he was feeling uncertain about what he'd done. It was a time of intense heartache; I knew I should be fully committed to what God was saying to me, but my heart was still divided. I found it unbearable to reflect on the pain that we were each experiencing, but I also knew my heart was focused on loving the one person it shouldn't at that time. I felt like a complete and utter mess; divided and deconstructed. At one point, my mum commented that I needed to take charge of my life as I was making myself ill. I was totally in limbo and felt completely helpless – and hopeless.

> I felt like a complete and utter mess; divided and deconstructed.

An ongoing process

I found it hard listening to the well-meaning voices who told me that I should simply go back to Steve. I knew that was what I *ought* to do – I just needed my heart and head in alignment before I could even consider it. I knew there was no point in rushing it, as we would both be left in the same situation as before, two broken and saddened people who would continue to hurt one another. I needed God's healing hand. For me, that process was kickstarted when the person who eventually counselled me spoke to me on the phone. After our initial conversation had finished, I realized that I had come away with a new sense of peace – and hope for my life. As I reflected on why that might be, I discovered that it was because she had listened to me, validated where I was at and at no time pressurized me with 'ought tos'. She recognized the deep hurt and healing that needed to take place, and graciously didn't rush me through that.

The process took time and I had many down days as well as those when I felt more positive. Throughout it all, one of the phrases I can remember God saying to me over and over again was that I was the apple of his eye – see Psalm 17:8. It was at the point of actually accepting that that I feel I truly surrendered everything to God for the first time (I thought I had many times before, but often it isn't until life is stripped right back that you can see things as they truly are).

I had three months staying with my parents, during which there were moments when Steve came to visit when I would desperately try not to feel numb, knowing God had spoken to me about the fact that I was meant to be with him. I knew I wanted to make it work with him, knew I needed to for my own sanity and for our future – and yet there were times when feelings for him came . . . and times when they didn't. I also found night-time so difficult, as I would be plagued with unhelpful dreams. While it was a most frustrating, isolating and bewildering time, I did experience incredible grace from both Steve and God. They each allowed me space and time, but also sat and listened to me when I spoke of what was going on in my head and heart. Eventually, Steve and I spent a week with the wonderful woman who had been so helpful on the phone and her husband. Each day we had individual counselling with them, as they worked through deep inner healing with us separately. They never sugar-coated things, nor did they rush through or push us to accept the resolution they would have been praying for. They simply gave us the safe space to recognize and work through the broken parts of our hearts. With tender, Spirit-whispered prompts, they gently guided us through a process that was intensely painful but also really freeing.

Looking back over my journals from that time, I was coming face to face with who I thought I was, realizing I had shut myself down emotionally, recognizing that I kept myself busy to prove myself worthy of love and, most of all, admitting that I felt my twenties had been a wasteland – a time of utter loss, loneliness and waste. God spoke directly into that, taking me to Joel 2:25: 'I will repay you for the years the locusts have eaten.' I got to a place of releasing the anguish and trusting God again for my future and for my marriage. I also took the step of forgiving Steve for perpetuating my feelings of loneliness and for making me feel like I wasn't as important as his job for all those years, as well as taking responsibility for how I had dwelt on those feelings, allowing them to grow and fester.

> I got to a place of releasing the anguish and trusting God again for my future and for my marriage.

Nearing the end of the week, I felt able to make the decision to recommit to Steve, and we had a beautiful moment, just between the four of us, renewing our marriage vows. It was made even more poignant because the man had been the pastor who had married us in the first place. There we were, a decade later, having been devastated and still tending to our wounds, but now determined to work alongside the Holy Spirit to put in foundations that would strengthen us going forward (something we had never had the chance to do early on in our marriage – more on that in Chapter 3).

Of course, while that might seem like a fairytale ending to a tough story, the reality was that it was hugely hard work – and still is. Back then we had to readjust to living with one another, learning to prefer one another again, choosing to reject the pain when it tried to engulf again (which it did, over and over). And we had to deal with the fact that we could look out of our back windows and see the house where the man I had trusted in lived.

There were times I was simply furious – mad at the fact that I still had to be in close vicinity to someone who had caused so much hurt. In my heart, I wanted the four of us to be reconciled – I think that was partly my inner being desperately trying to resolve what I had been through. To suggest it to Steve was quite preposterous. And yet I did, quite often. It was R.T. Kendall's book *Total Forgiveness*[2] that finally settled in my heart that you can forgive and still not reconcile – that sometimes to do so would be unwise (even harmful). (See Chapter 4 for more on this.)

In certain moments, everything we were dealing with seemed too much – for both of us. For me, there were moments of such deep intense pain, when the enormity of what had happened and what I'd lost (that rejection again) hit me afresh, and I would simply break down and howl. In those times, Steve would simply hold me and reassure me of his love, even when I lashed out like a wild animal, totally absorbed by my primeval pain. What an intensely difficult, incredible thing for him to do.

There were also the beautiful moments when the enormity of what God had stepped in and done hit us too – that still happens every so often, as we are overwhelmed by his grace in our lives.

Grace Chooses to Trust

Love . . . always protects, always trusts, always hopes, always perseveres.

1 Corinthians 13:6–7

Today we seem to be in a period when global politics has struggled to earn any sense of integrity in manifestoes, promises and even in democratic elections; trust is in short supply. In fact, trust in politicians, the media, big corporations – and perhaps even in each other – is at an all-time low. There is a trust deficit in our culture. Yet trust is vital if we are to work together.

The *Oxford English Dictionary* states that trust means: 'Firm belief in the reliability, truth, or ability of someone or something.'[1] It is a huge deal, when you feel that trust has been broken, to actually choose to place your trust in another person again.

> Trust is risky. It opens our hearts to potential hurt, disappointment and pain.

Trust is risky. It opens our hearts to potential hurt, disappointment and pain, but it is also the only path to a relationship that has any depth at all. Trust is a non-negotiable. In entrusting our hearts to one another, we are handing over our most precious possession (the thing we are actually commanded to guard above all else, Prov. 4:23) to someone else. That is not easy – particularly if that person has betrayed our trust or disappointed us. And yet, it is something we must do as the first step in building a relationship. Choosing to trust is choosing to be vulnerable, choosing to be open again – but also choosing to allow another's love into your own heart.

Claire: I spoke in the last chapter about getting to the point that I could speak out that I trusted God once more with our marriage. That was a huge step for me – and the most important one. We each have to trust that God is with us in our marriages, even when we are going through really difficult experiences. And Steve had to make that choice to trust me again, even though I had broken his trust and our marriage vows. But I also had to take that giant leap of trusting Steve enough to speak those vows once more and, ultimately, move back home.

Steve: If trust is a key foundation of any relationship, it must therefore also be the foundation of our relationship with God. We are told that without faith [trusting in God's character and promises] it is impossible to please God (Heb. 11:6) and Proverbs 3:5 challenges us to: 'Trust in the LORD with all your heart and lean not on your own understanding'. That is often easier said than done. So often we lean on our own understanding and base our decisions on our current circumstances and what we can actually see. And yet, with God, our understanding falls so far short. His ways are so much higher than our ways and so we simply cannot rely on our understanding. We have to rely on what we believe is true of him – that he is good and is sovereign over all things.

We need to believe this is true in the good times but also in the painful times. In the seasons of plenty and the seasons of barrenness. Whenever we are tempted to doubt God, we can usually trace it back to doubting one of these truths.

As we were rebuilding our marriage and learning to trust each other again one verse that helped was Romans 8:28: 'We know that in all things God works for the good of those who love him, who have been called according to his purpose.' It was that phrase 'all things' that arrested me: was God able to work for the good even through our mistakes? Yes. Was he able to continue his purposes in us and through us despite the mess we had made of our marriage? Yes!

One person in the Old Testament that had to choose to trust God and not lean on his own understanding was Joseph. His story is found in Genesis 37–50. You could argue that he got into a mess of his own making by bragging to his brothers about his God-given dreams and how they would one day bow down to him. He certainly was foolish. And yet, after narrowly escaping being murdered by his brothers and instead being sold into slavery, his trust in God somehow didn't waiver. He was entrusted with a wealthy ruler's household, yet, ironically, was wrongfully accused of abusing that trust, which landed him in prison. Let down by his family, let down by his slave master, he was let down yet again. This time it was by a fellow prisoner – the cupbearer to the king. Joseph interpreted a dream for him, telling him he would be restored to his noble position. In return, the cupbearer promised to put in a good word to Pharaoh. Yet the newly restored cupbearer forgot his promise to Joseph. It was two more long years before he finally remembered Joseph, when Pharaoh himself needed someone to interpret some disturbing dreams he had been having. Giving credit to God, Joseph successfully interpreted Pharaoh's dreams, describing a coming famine with a call to prepare. As a reward, Pharaoh promoted Joseph to second-in-command of Egypt. From this influential position, God then used Joseph's wisdom and ways to save a nation from famine (Gen. 41).

Joseph refused to let go of the truth that God is good and that he is sovereign over all things. He was so convinced of the purposes of God working through even his hardships and betrayals that he was able to say to his brothers: 'You intended to harm me, but God intended it for good to accomplish what is now being done, the saving of many lives' (Gen. 50:20).

It is often said that trust needs to be earned, yet, while there is some truth in that, it is not the full story. With a perfect God, we can look back on his past promises; indeed so much of Scripture is remembering the trustworthiness of our God. Like Joseph, we can gain comfort from the fact that he was faithful in the past and he will continue to be faithful in the future. He is the same, yesterday, today and forever (Heb. 13:8). But what about trusting broken, imperfect people again? Do we wait until they have a long, proven reliable track record before we are prepared to trust them once more?

One of the most beautiful parts of Joseph's story for me is the way he reconciled with his brothers. Genesis 42 describes how they travelled from their famine-stricken home in Canaan to Egypt, having heard that there was food there. On meeting Joseph, they had no clue that this powerful Egyptian ruler was in fact their brother, who they had sold into slavery years before. Joseph initially hid his identity and, instead, tested their integrity – you could argue by using deceptive means (Gen. 43–44). Yet he saw that they had changed when his older brother, Judah, put his life on the line for their little brother, Benjamin. Joseph finally revealed who he truly was and, through tears, reconciled with them (Gen. 45:1–15).

Joseph had both the position and the motive to really make his brothers pay for their past mistakes. After being let down time and time again by people he trusted, he could so easily have hardened his heart and refused to trust anyone ever again. Yet, after seeing how his brothers had changed, he chose to trust them again. He didn't wait years for them to prove themselves or make atonement – he simply opened his heart once more.

When you have experienced hurt or betrayal, and yet you have seen a repentant heart, there comes a time when you have to, proactively and intentionally, choose to trust again. To choose to build again. To learn to be vulnerable again.

Re-laying foundations

Claire: Once we were fully back together, we knew that we needed to find a more local couple to counsel us – it took a little while but eventually, through enquiries to our previous church and lists of Christian counsellors, we found people who weren't too far away and who could start seeing us quickly. We didn't know this couple, but they were incredibly gentle, oozed God's grace to us and immediately put us at ease so that we could be totally honest – and trust them with our struggles and pain as we tried to outwork our marriage and re-lay the foundations. That's not to say I didn't struggle – a lot. I found the first bit of 'homework' they set us so difficult: 'Think back to when you were engaged and tell each other what you loved about one another.' When they said that, the pain immediately reared up again – and telling Steve what I loved about him was the last thing I wanted to do!

To be honest, while my heart had been softened by Steve's overwhelming love and acceptance of me, I hadn't had a rush of positive deep emotion since the renewal of the vows. At this point, it all seemed like daily decisions and hard work – and a lot of difficult emotions rising up. But I knew I had to persevere through all of that, as I still had a broken heart that needed time to mend. I know that sometimes God sweeps away all the pain miraculously . . . but, more often than not, he doesn't. There is a long-term process in unpacking it and letting it go, and God does deep soul-work in that time. It can be excruciating – and annoying!

We could both have given up quite easily at that point and yet we knew we had to clear the way and start to build again. We realized that we'd never had the chance or made the effort to build in strong foundations in the first place. When we'd had an offer for pre-marriage classes I'd turned them down, as I would have had to attend by myself (Steve's work pattern simply wouldn't have facilitated him attending). And, once married, we were already in the routine of Steve working around the clock, so there was no time to actually think about and systematically work on our marriage. So much of our behaviour and interactions were reactive – and too often done ungraciously, as we were so exhausted all of the time.

We now have the joy and privilege of doing pre-marital counselling sessions for couples in our church and, whenever we see a new couple, we realize again how much work marriage is, and the many things we have let slip over time. It is so, so important to work on our marriages regularly – I would say daily – because they can too easily end up on the bottom of the priority pile, and that is something that kills a relationship.

While this can all seem like a lot of hard work, the truth is, passivity and resignation that 'this is just the way things are' are big killers of the joy that can be found in marriage. We each married our partner because we trusted that they were the one we were meant to journey through life with and, whatever point we may be at right now, taking the time to remind ourselves of that belief and acting in faith out of it, shows us, our partners and God that we mean business.

Rebuilding trust

While we each had to make the decision to trust the other, we also knew that the rebuilding of trust doesn't happen overnight. It takes space – and a huge amount of grace. That decision had to happen every day, over and over – and despite an incredible amount of pain. As Steve says, trust is actually a proactive choice – we have to intentionally place our trust in another.

> Trust is actually a proactive choice – we have to intentionally place our trust in another.

When a betrayal happens, the onus is usually put on the betrayer to make amends. Sympathy, prayers and help often get poured over the betrayed – and yet, in truth, both need that level of support. There will be an underlying reason for the betrayal: it could be due to an ongoing battle with sin, such as a porn addiction or lust, but may be due to something like the response to past pain (which, in my instance, caused me to become bitter and sinful as a result). But both betrayer and betrayed are wounded people, and both need deep healing as well as the courage to choose to trust the person who has hurt them the most.

While this isn't an example from a marriage, let me explain what I mean about the betrayer being a wounded person too, by looking at when Peter disowned Jesus. In Matthew 26:69–75 we read of how Peter did the exact thing he vowed to Jesus he would never do. And then, when the cock crowed for that third time, how did he respond? He 'went outside and wept bitterly'. The knowledge of his sin, of the fact that he behaved in the very way he said he would never behave, overcame him and he simply fell apart under the weight of it.

When David was rebuked by Nathan for his adulterous relationship with Bathsheba (and his horrific behaviour afterwards to try and cover his tracks), he was still quite oblivious to what he had done (see 2 Sam. 12:1–6). But when Nathan pointed out that he had been describing David, David was overwhelmed by his sin too. He immediately stated 'I have sinned against the LORD' (v.13), and fasted and pleaded for the life of his son. Knowing this his son's death was caused by his sin would have been a wound that cut so deeply.

Having lived through our own situation, and knowing the experiences of others too, it seems to us that as churches we can be guilty of only extending grace to the betrayed and not the betrayer. Is that how God measures out his grace? Just to those who he feels are deserving of it? If that was the case, none of us would ever be at the receiving end of it! How grateful we are that his grace is a 'gift of God' (Eph. 2:8), as none of us could ever earn it ourselves.

We both desperately needed prayer, continual support – and accountability (see Chapters 8, 10, 11 and 12). For now, we had to realize that we each needed to extend grace to one another in a very practical way by choosing to give the other the benefit of the doubt each day. We would talk deep issues over, thereby showing that we were willing to work on them together, rather than hiding away those bits of us that were still hurting. It was a very painful process, but if we had simply waited until we'd each felt that the other had done enough to earn our trust again, when would it have ever been enough?

If we are waiting for the other to earn the right to be trusted again, how do we measure that? Presumably, we will be constantly looking and measuring them up against our own standard, which will result in us feeling justified in withholding our trust. If both partners are doing that, they will never meet together. (The truth is, in such instances, we are simply blind to our own faults, as none of us is perfect.) However difficult it may be to begin with (in whatever situation as this can happen regularly with much smaller situations), extending grace to our partner in this way is the only means of actually building that trust back up.

Redefining our purpose

Perhaps you were taught this in the marriage preparation classes you went to, but it wasn't until we were in counselling that we first heard the notion of having a vision for our marriage. Up until the point that our marriage imploded, we had simply had our heads down, plodding through each year. I would say, every so often, that I didn't feel I could continue with life as it was, but then we didn't feel like we had any other choice. So, with some resignation and sadness, we would simply continue as we were, pushing down the pain and regrets, only for them to explode out of us at unexpected moments and in deeply unhelpful ways.

Strangely, we knew that we had been called to be together but we had never actually worked out what for, what God's specific purpose was for us. If I'm honest, I guess my romantic ideals meant that I had viewed Steve as my 'soul mate', the one who would bring me happiness. Of course, that is totally unbiblical – and untrue! Only God can bring us that deep, lasting joy. When Jesus spoke to the woman at the well in John 4, he knew that she'd had five husbands but was still looking for lasting peace and joy. What he offered was water that would satisfy way beyond the physical thirst we feel: 'Everyone who drinks this water will be thirsty again, but whoever drinks the water I give them will never thirst. Indeed, the water I give them will become in them a spring of water welling up to eternal life' (vv.13–14). When we look to him to fill us up, not only we ourselves but our marriages (and other relationships) will benefit too.

Marriage isn't supposed to be about what we get out of it – or even what we give to it. Marriage is a reflection of God's relationship with his church and, as we talked about in the introduction, it has a much bigger purpose than we may realize. So, we can each know that God's purpose for our marriage is for us to reflect his glory (and it is also a way that he sanctifies us). But we are all individuals, and our marriages are all very different – because God is a creative, expansive God and we reflect different facets of his glory. While we can know a general purpose, God also has a specific one for each of our marriages too.

At counselling we were taught to intentionally sit down and prayerfully consider what our vision was for our marriage, and then to regularly revisit it and firstly see how well we thought we were doing, but also see whether we needed to tweak anything. In one of the 'homeworks' we were set, we were asked to come up with a set of values for our marriage and then to write a vision statement. Just to give you a little flavour of what I mean, here are a couple of our values:

Openness: Be open and honest with one another and talk things through whenever necessary.

Friendship: Learn not to take ourselves too seriously all the time and to have fun together – simply enjoying each other's company.

We have found that the values and vision statement have become useful markers, measuring sticks even, for us to check against every so often.

> We have learned that our ministry has often been birthed in our deepest pain.

Interestingly, through our most painful experiences, we have seen God birth a new aspect to our purpose together – encouraging true authenticity and giving a safe space to other couples to be honest about their relationships. Often it is those very painful experiences that not only shape us the most deeply, but also provide the means for God reaching out to others through us. God never wastes any of our tears, any of our pain. We have learned that our ministry has often been birthed in our deepest pain.

While I could never have imagined Steve becoming a pastor, and I certainly baulked at becoming a pastor's wife, today I get such a buzz, and experience real joy, when we are truly working together in whatever capacity – whether it be in a church service, seeing a couple for marriage preparation or one of us is looking after the kids so the other can prepare for their next speaking engagement.

Learning to trust God, and each other, in the pain

Malcolm Harris explains how both he and his wife Kim had been married previously, and that after a while, old patterns of behaviour began to surface in their relationship, causing a lack of intimacy between them. As they learned to open up and trust God more, they have been able to change, and today enjoy a stronger marriage as a result.

I married Carol (not her real name) in 1984. We were both Christians, but from the start we had an extremely difficult and volatile marriage. Looking back, we both brought a lot of baggage into our marriage from dysfunctional childhoods that worked as powerful hindrances to a good marriage. I grew up with a fear of rejection and abandonment; my mum and dad were never happy and subsequently separated and divorced. I craved love and attention. Carol grew up in a very controlling family and struggled with her sexual identity.

Having witnessed the breakdown of my parents' marriage I was determined to make it work, but, after ten years of a largely loveless marriage, Carol left to live with another lady she had met in our church. She took our two young boys (aged 6 and 4) with her. The sense of betrayal and hurt was overwhelming. Although I kept going to work every day, looking back, I had something of a breakdown. I cried every day for a year and life was painful and joyless. Even when I had my boys for a weekend, there was little joy because I knew I had to give them back again. Carol completely cut me off, and I was clinging on to keep contact and be a father to my boys. The love of my twin brother and a close friend enabled me to get through this time.

Kim had a boyfriend when she was 15. It was a volatile relationship, and they separated. But he became a Christian and,
soon after, got back in touch with Kim. She visited the church
he attended in south London and thought they were all mad,
but after a few visits she was really taken by the love and joy
she found in the people. She committed her life to Jesus Christ
and encountered the love of God herself. Kim's relationship with
her boyfriend was restored and they subsequently married. Sadly,
Kim's husband contracted cancer and, after living with the disease for six years, he died in 1995. Kim was left with four boys
(16, 14, 13 and 10) and a lot of debt. I knew Kim's first husband
(he was a dear friend). He was sick at the time Carol left me, and
I visited him in hospital. I could see Kim was an amazing wife and
mother; she worked every day in the market to earn an income
and looked after and cared for her husband and children.

Deep wounds take over the joy

After her husband died, Kim and I kept in touch, just as friends,
but after three years love blossomed. Neither of us had believed
we could be happy again, but we fell deeply in love and we were
overwhelmed by the grace of God. We were so happy and were
quickly married in May 1998.

While we had a very difficult time trying to blend our families,
the early years of our marriage were in many respects blissful. But
in July 2001, Kim's third son was killed in a road traffic accident,
just before his 18th birthday. Our family and faith were turned
upside down. Kim turned to drink to cover the searing pain of
loss; my fears of rejection and abandonment quickly dominated
once again. Kim's default position was to be independent and
insular; to just get on with it. Our deep wounds and coping mech-
anisms kept us from the intimacy we craved. We kept going to

church, but we were struggling in our relationship. One night, I was crying silently in my bed, wondering whether I could carry on. In Psalm 13:1 the psalmist cries out to God: 'Will you forget me forever?' I used it to cry out to God myself, and felt him say to me: 'Another six months and things will start to turn around'.

Pursued by the love and grace of God

We moved to a new house in April 2006 and joined a more charismatic church. It was at this time Kim felt God say to her, 'Will you declare that I am good all the time and worship me?' To do so meant letting go of the pain, disappointment and loss, but Kim decided to trust God. This was not a process that had been easily nor quickly arrived at. People had indicated that the grief process may take a year or two but, in reality, for Kim it was more like five or six years, during which time she had been grappling with various emotions including confusion, disappointment, guilt and anger (in some ways grief still raises its head). Most of these emotions were expressed primarily to God, but they also impacted our family life. On the day God spoke so clearly to her, Kim came to the point of understanding that he was looking for complete surrender, even of the things she didn't understand. Raising her hands in surrender and worship, she felt some of the burden she had been carrying fall away; a new freedom came to worship God and trust him. Looking back, this was the grace of God: a realization that freedom comes in surrender, not in holding on to our wounds and hurts. The Bible tells us God is love, and love always pursues and seeks the best for the other. This seems too good to be true, but it has become truth for us.

Even so, we still went through times where our old patterns of behaviour came to the fore; we would in our respective ways feel unloved and unappreciated. For me, old feelings of being alone and needing to try harder surfaced. I could spiral, go into myself and feel self-pity, wondering why Kim couldn't see my position and do something positive to make it different. For Kim, she would become independent and just get on with life her way. We were left in a position where we needed the opposite from the way the other was behaving and it was hard to trust one another with our hearts during this time.

While we have legitimate needs in the marriage that our spouse can meet, I began to recognize that I was looking for Kim to meet love needs in me that she wasn't equipped, nor intended, to meet. Indeed, I saw that she could never meet them. Such deep love needs could only be met by God himself. Although I had been a Christian many years, I began a journey of surrendering more fully to God. This has had the effect of encouraging Kim to also give herself more fully to God. This has been liberating to both of us, and I see this as the grace of God: as we have trusted God with more of ourselves, the impact has been that we have been able to show deeper love and trust to one another.

While we still have times when the old patterns of behaviour kick in, these episodes are now rarer, and we recognize them more readily for what they are. We have come to understand that we are not alone: God is totally trustworthy and true to his word, so will never leave us or forsake us.

I am now less interested in having my own egotistical needs met, since I have come to realize there is no deep happiness or contentment in them. Any joy or happiness that they brought was only temporary and fleeting. We are finding our true selves in God.

We are still on this journey of learning to trust God and each other, giving ourselves completely to him and learning how to give ourselves sacrificially to one another. I would like to say that the transformation had been a quick one, but it hasn't; it seems that it is a lifelong pilgrimage. But it is so worth it. We have discovered that God loves us in our weaknesses and vulnerability, and that as we have recognized such failings and released them to God, their power to dominate our lives has diminished. Moreover, the love of God and a sense of wellbeing has increased.

Of course, the passage of time in a marriage brings its own changes. The body changes and so does life (for example, we are now grandparents). However, it is true to say that we are now more satisfied in God and each other than we have ever been. Psalm 16:2 has really spoken to me in recent days: 'apart from you [God] I have no good thing'. Everything that is good is a gift, including the gift of our marriage.

Over to you

- Discuss together what foundations you believe you have built your marriage on. Is there anything you need to pull down in order to build firmer foundations instead?
- Take some time to talk and pray through what your vision is for your marriage. If you have already got a vision statement, revisit it and check whether you are still on track. If you've never written one, brainstorm the values you hold dear in your marriage and then take time to write a vision statement.
- Reflect on whether there are any areas of broken trust in your marriage. If so, bring those before God and ask for his help to work through them together honestly and with grace.

Grace Extends Forgiveness

Forgive as the Lord forgave you.

Colossians 3:13

Steve: If choosing to trust again is the first step in rebuilding a relationship then walking the path of forgiveness is the next . . . and the next! Because forgiving someone is never a one-off. I believe, like trust, forgiveness needs to be an intentional choice. In fact, it is a daily choice and absolutely vital if we are to move forward.

In the early days of rebuilding our marriage I used to question whether Claire was truly sorry for her actions. I would try and gauge whether she had an 'appropriate level of remorse' at what she had done. Did she deserve my forgiveness? Did she think it was actually all my fault? Looking back now I see how incredibly self-righteous (and ignorant) I was being. I needed to learn that forgiveness has nothing to do with the other person's level of repentance or even regret. In fact forgiveness has very little to do with the other person at all, but it has everything to do with the state of our own hearts. Forgiveness says, I refuse to allow that person's offence to have a hold over me – in the way I feel about the situation but also the way I feel about the person. Forgiveness is not about letting someone off the hook but about releasing ourselves from the bondage of resentment and bitterness.

> Forgiveness is not about letting someone off the hook but about releasing ourselves from the bondage of resentment and bitterness.

Pride, once again, plays a damaging role in our ability to forgive. If we keep holding on to a sense of superiority or start grading sins, 'I may have done this but I have never done what you did', then we will always struggle to forgive. That is where a true understanding of the Gospel is so vital.

Jesus taught us to ask for forgiveness *as we forgive those who sin against us* (see Luke 11:4). Our forgiveness of others is always in the context of the incredible forgiveness God has given us. As I contemplated the grace God had shown me through Jesus, I was compelled to forgive Claire – how could I not? Passages like Matthew 18:21–35, 'The parable of the unmerciful servant', really helped me. Jesus told this story in response to Peter asking him how many times we need to forgive. Or to put it another way, when do you finally say that you have run out of grace? Peter suggested perhaps seven times. Jesus replied, try nearer seventy times seven! In the story Jesus described a servant who was let off a huge sum of money – an amount that would have taken decades to earn. As he fell on his knees begging, his master let him off the whole lot. Yet as this servant left, he bumped into a fellow servant who owed him a day's wages. Having just been let off a lifetime's debt, he grabbed the other servant by the neck and demanded he pay back what he owed. Showing no mercy when this fellow servant pleaded for patience, he had him thrown into prison. On hearing the news, the master was justifiably enraged and instead handed the unmerciful servant over to the jailers to be tortured.

Jesus' words hit home: 'This is how my heavenly Father will treat each of you unless you forgive your brother or sister from your heart' (v.35).

My debt of gratitude towards God could and should be directed towards Claire in forgiveness. 'Forgive as the Lord forgave you,' says Colossians 3:13. How could I withhold from her what God has so freely given to me? That's not to say there weren't daily struggles with this. I had to keep reminding myself of these truths and keep aligning my heart and mind with them.

We forgive others because of Jesus. We learn to forgive much when we reflect on what we ourselves have been forgiven of. Rather than spiralling into a pit of guilt, humbly acknowledging what God has done for us is important, as it motivates our forgiveness. Remember: 'as far as the east is from the west, so far has he removed our transgressions from us' (Ps. 103:12).

Claire: I spoke of R.T. Kendall's book *Total Forgiveness*[1] previously. It certainly had a huge impact on me, probably because it spoke so openly and honestly about the wrestling that I recognized I had experienced in my own heart. I found that I was able to forgive Steve for past hurt and so we could move on together, but I kept being overwhelmed by feelings of anger that the other person involved had basically been let off the hook – he'd got away with trampling on our hearts and then leaving.

I seemed to be trapped in a cycle: we would make headway then something would happen that would trigger the feelings of rejection and hurt afresh, and I would get consumed by the unfairness of it all. How dare he get off without punishment! In brutal honesty, I wanted revenge for how he had made me feel. (The Bible tells us that it is not down to us to judge, and that God is the one who will avenge where necessary – see Rom. 12:19. In practice, this is not always easy to do.)

I was challenged by the book (and God) to keep quiet about the things I felt were unfair, but in doing so what I was suppressing began to eat me up inside. It was only when I recognized the truth of what R.T. was saying about peace and guilt that I began to realize that *I* was the one I was hurting when I refused to extend forgiveness – the other person had no idea of my struggle and it certainly had no impact on him. I finally began to understand that forgiveness is not about approving, excusing or denying what he had done, but rather about releasing myself from a burden (as Steve had learned before me). When I made the conscious effort to forgive, which was incredibly painful at the time, I experienced God's peace and was set free from the prison that was, in fact, of my own making.

While that was a total revelation at the time, I can't say that I instantly conquered the situation and forgave fully and totally forever. It was certainly a process, with me having to choose that forgiveness each time the feelings of injustice and guilt threatened to engulf me again – just like Steve described above. But through the gift of R.T.'s book, I had learned that that choice, however difficult, meant the difference between being engulfed by bitterness and enjoying God's peace.

There was one part of what R.T. taught that it took me a long time to master. While he talked about ensuring we don't talk about a person's offence to anyone, he also suggested that being able to pray a blessing over them was a good way of knowing we had truly forgiven them. While I learned to do the former, biting my tongue at times when around friends who had witnessed what had happened (and who, deep down, I wanted to understand my point of view), it was a much bigger deal for me to pray a blessing over him and his wife. I had learned to face

> Being able to pray a blessing over someone shows that we have not allowed bitterness to take root.

up to why I wanted to talk to others about it: it wasn't because I needed the outlet for myself; it was because I wanted him to go down in other people's estimation. That sounds awful – and it is – but I don't think I'm alone in battling that same desire at times. However, God is not impressed by it at all. Being able to pray a blessing over someone shows that we have not allowed bitterness to take root.

Learning the importance of self-forgiveness

I said earlier that it took me quite a while to truly understand the depth of my own sin. I was too wrapped up in my pain and anguish. But, having done so, it could have been so easy to have become totally enveloped in another negative emotion: guilt. I think sometimes we can believe that we deserve to feel bad about our actions; that somehow that intensity of guilt is good because it drives home our need for forgiveness. And yet . . . while we may ask for, and receive, forgiveness from God and from our partner, often we withhold it from ourselves.

In the process of sinning, we not only let God and others down, we let ourselves down too, so we need to learn self-forgiveness in order to move on. To say we accept God's forgiveness and yet choose to cling on to guilt, means that we haven't actually fully understood his forgiveness. Jesus said: 'Do not judge, and you will not be judged. Do not condemn, and you will not be condemned. Forgive, and you will be forgiven' (Luke 6:37). There is no disclaimer telling us that while we need to do this to others we shouldn't do it to ourselves. We are included in his commands.

I used to read Paul's words in 1 Corinthians 4:3–4 as rather arrogant: 'I care very little if I am judged by you or by any human court; indeed, I do not even judge myself. My conscience is clear, but that does not make me innocent. It is the Lord who judges me.' But actually, he was fully arrested by the depth of his sin on the Damascus Road (Acts 9) – and then enjoyed the total forgiveness of God. He knew that God alone is the one who has the right to judge. So he had accepted full forgiveness from God, which included forgiving himself (he no longer judged himself), just as Jesus instructed us to. This meant he could go on to fulfil his calling, as he expressed in 1 Timothy 1:15–16: 'Christ Jesus came into the world to save sinners – of whom I am the worst. But for that very reason I was shown mercy so that in me, the worst of sinners, Christ Jesus might display his immense patience as an example for those who would believe in him and receive eternal life.'

I do recognize that forgiving ourselves isn't necessarily an easy thing to do at all – it is far more natural for us to continue to be critical of ourselves, to be harder towards ourselves than we are on others, and to refuse to extend grace to ourselves. It seems to be an almost subconscious thing – deep inside we feel we need to continue to be punished and so we play that out without really being aware of it. But that actually reflects badly

> It is far more natural for us to continue to be critical of ourselves, to be harder towards ourselves than we are on others.

on our faith in the finished work of Jesus on the cross. We need to recognize that when we truly acknowledge our sin, his blood totally covers us. This means that any guilt we feel after repentance is false guilt, and it would be a sin to hold on to that.

God wants us to move past sin – but of course the devil wants us locked into it, or if we move beyond that, into unforgiveness, as that means we will get trapped in the feelings of guilt. But, as the Living Bible eloquently puts it: 'A further reason for forgiveness is to keep from being outsmarted by Satan, for we know what he is trying to do' (2 Cor. 2:11).

I couldn't have moved on to fully embrace our marriage again if I hadn't extended forgiveness to myself as well as the other parties involved. I would have carried a massive pile of baggage with me, which would have weighed us both down. I also couldn't have loved Steve in the way that I have been called to. The Bible teaches 'love your neighbour as yourself' (Lev. 19:18; Matt. 19:19) – but that means we need to love ourselves well in order to be able to do that. Although so many of us find this difficult today, God created us to love ourselves; we cannot do that if we are harbouring unforgiveness towards ourselves.

I have talked about Paul, but there is another biblical character I want to bring in here. He has really impacted me as I've worked through my own history, and so he featured in *Taking Off the Mask* too. Peter really blew it didn't he? If anyone had a reason not to forgive themselves it is him – denying our Saviour so soon after he had been warned that he would do so, which he vehemently denied would happen (see Mark 14:27–31, 66–72).

How do you come back from such a mistake? By accepting Jesus' forgiveness and extending it to yourself too (John 21:15–17). Jesus called out Peter's mission on earth, 'feed my sheep' (v.17), and in Acts 2 we see Peter confidently explaining to the crowd what was happening on the Day of Pentecost, and who Jesus truly was. It is interesting to note that, while Luke's description of what Jesus said to Peter at the Last Supper is shorter, he included the vital detail of Jesus praying for him:

'I have prayed for you, Simon, that your faith may not fail. And when you have turned back, strengthen your brothers' (Luke 22:32). We can rest assured that Jesus is doing the same, interceding on our behalf, today: 'Who then is the one who condemns? No one. Christ Jesus who died – more than that, who was raised to life – is at the right hand of God and is also interceding for us' (Rom. 8:34).

Often we stumble with forgiving ourselves because we have learned a pattern of being self-critical. This may stem right back to experiences in our childhood, where we learned how to talk to ourselves based on how our primary caregivers spoke to us. In an attempt to push us to achieve, sometimes caregivers inadvertently fuelled our inner voice with negativity. Unfortunately, whether our childhood was happy or difficult, psychologists have discovered that our inner voice remembers negative words far more than positive ones.[2] This can be why we find it so much easier to put ourselves down than forgive and encourage ourselves. It can also make it difficult for us to accept our partner's love, and to believe that we can be forgiven when we have done something wrong.

If you know that you have a pattern of being overly critical of yourself, then it is important to take the time to ask God to help you recognize when you are continuing to beat yourself up about something he has already forgiven you for. You can refuse to dwell on the sin and openly resist the lie that you still can't forgive yourself by choosing to state, by faith, that you do. You can also replace the lie with the truth that you stand forgiven by Jesus. This can all take time to learn to do, but it is worth putting in the practise, as otherwise you can be weighed down by feelings of unworthiness, which is not how God views you at all. The Bible says: 'Resist the devil, and he will flee from you' (Jas 4:7) and we are also told to 'be transformed by the renewing of your mind' (Rom. 12:2). This is vital for self-forgiveness. You owe it to yourself, your partner, your marriage and God himself to take the time to work on this area if you recognize it as a problem in your life.

Self-forgiveness does not puff us up: we still recognize that we are works in progress and need God's grace each and every day. Self-forgiveness also doesn't give us an excuse to simply carry on sinning. Paul had strong words to say about that in Romans 6:1–2: 'What shall we say, then? Shall we go on sinning, so that grace may increase? By no means! We are those who have died to sin; how can we live in it any longer?' This is about extending the same level of forgiveness to ourselves that God does – we are simply agreeing with him.

Fast from recrimination and feast on forgiveness

Penelope Swithinbank talks about how she and her husband of over thirty years, Kim, became like strangers – and how forgiveness was the key to them finding each other again.

We'd drifted apart, my husband and I. There were days when I'd look at him and wonder if I knew him at all. After more than three decades of what on the whole had been a good marriage, I seemed now to be married to a stranger. He was desperately unhappy, I knew that, although now I know that the unhappiness was even deeper and darker than I had ever imagined. There was buried pain from the past, including that of being sent away to boarding school at the age of seven, and there was the recent pain of his mother's unexpected death without the sense of rejection and abandonment from being sent away ever having been talked about or resolved. There was an abject sense of failure that had dogged him all his life; and there was the current pain of being stuck in a job that was causing a lot of pain, anxiety and distress. A job that was actually full-time ordained ministry, in a church where neither of us was feeling at home and where we each sensed we were not a good 'fit' at all.

Trying to persevere

We were . . . are . . . Christians. Perhaps the sacrifice of contentment and fulfilment was what we were being called to and what we were supposed to learn to bring to God for him to sort out? To walk out after less than a year would perhaps be running away, or not being good enough Christians or strong enough in our faith? Would people judge us and condemn us if we left?

So we didn't leave; we thought we were to persevere and persist and be stoically 'Christian'.

And in the process, we each sank deeper and deeper into misery and pain, exacerbated by the horrific accident in which I witnessed my mother knocked over by an out-of-control car and her life tragically ended there on the road.

The pain and the misery of our lives did not draw us closer to each other, nor closer to the Lord. We each clammed up, shut down, turned away. From each other and from the Lord. It became what we later called the 'dosi-do', the dance of our lives where we seemed to turn inwards whenever there was stress and trouble and pain; we pushed it all down and pretended on the surface that everything was alright. We found other ways to cope or to numb the pain and turned our backs on each other.

There were failures, poor choices, bad decisions. The dark unhappiness led to a mental breakdown for my husband and severe PTSD for me. He suffered physical illnesses as well – in particular, a stroke. And so we drifted apart in every way possible, and it led eventually to a time of separation. A time to try to sort ourselves out with the help of God and the good friends he had blessed us with. A time for personal prayer and reflection, for learning the beginnings of forgiveness and trying to discover a way forward.

Time away

I decided I needed to go somewhere where I would be surrounded by the sense of God; somewhere I could be quiet to think and read and pray. I went to an Anglican convent in Monmouthshire, and a wonderful Spirit-filled nun, on listening to my story and sitting with me and praying for me, told me to stay in bed and rest as much as I needed. She advised me not to concern myself with the rhythm of chapel services but to come as and when I felt able, not to worry if I just sat and cried, and to go on long walks if I wanted to. The wonderful sense of freedom to just *be*, after the long dark years, was liberating.

One evening, sitting in the chapel and listening to the nuns singing, I gazed at the large crucifix hanging on the far wall and found words circling inside my head:

'Fast from recrimination and feast on forgiveness.'

I'm not sure, humanly speaking, where that came from. The Bible reading a few minutes earlier had included the word 'recrimination', and it was Lent so there was fasting among the nuns and guests. The words entered my mind and stayed there. 'Fast from recrimination' – oh, I was so good at recalling and remembering the hurts done to me. Not the ones I had inflicted, of course, just the ones done to me. Why should I forgive? Why should I forget? Look how much I've been hurt: this . . . and this . . . and that . . .

'Teach me, Lord, to fast from these moments, which like to play over and over in my head. Teach me to hear instead your voice of love and grace. Teach me, above all, to feast – feast! – on forgiveness. Teach me to welcome home the prodigal . . .'

Over my time at the convent, I read slowly through Henri Nouwen's book, *The Return of the Prodigal Son* and sat reflecting on the painting of the same name by Rembrandt that inspired the book. There was a large full-page reproduction of it in the book; the hands of the Father are clearly extended on to the back of the son, and Rembrandt painted not a pair of hands, but a male and a female hand, to show the different elements of the nature of God. They are pulling the son into the embrace, extending welcome and forgiveness and grace. The Father has been patiently watching and waiting; now, his love overflows and his hands express what is in his heart. Could God teach me to do the same? Did I even want him to? Probably not. Sometimes it's enjoyable to feast on recriminations and on hurts done to me. But that's not God's way; it's not what the words were telling me.

The eyes of the reproduction of Christ on the cross on the far end wall above the altar seemed to look straight down at me: 'Are you willing to be willing? Are you teachable? Could you *let me* love and forgive through your hands, your actions, your words?'

My tears fell. My heart beat faster and my hands opened as a gesture to show what I was barely able to give word to. 'Not my will, but yours, oh God. If this is what you're asking of me, make me willing to be willing.'

The second reading was from Mark 8, where Jesus tells his followers that they need to take up their cross and follow him. And again, words seemed to be going around in my mind, words that said I'd been carrying this cross of hurt and pain very begrudgingly. Instead, I was to ask not 'Why me?' but 'Why *not* me and what might I need to learn, and learn to be, in and through all of this?' Suddenly I caught a glimpse of what others might be carrying, a cross that perhaps humbles or hurts them. Perhaps in carrying my own cross, and in learning to fast from recrimination and feast on forgiveness, I might be able to hold up a light for others in their own darkness and support and encourage them.

The process of forgiveness

It would be nice if forgiveness could be a linear process – perhaps for some it is. But for my husband and me, it's not just the two-dimensional element of two people forgiving each other and then moving forward in tandem, it's almost more three dimen-sional. There's each of us, and then there's the process, which goes up and down, backwards and forwards. Usually, we each want to forgive, and sometimes it feels as though we really and truly have. But then comes a day, a situation or even just tired-ness, where one or other (or indeed both) doesn't even *want* to forgive, and it's all too easy to say something, or act, or not act in a way that is anything *but* forgiving. The recriminations are not far below the surface and may come out in how we behave or in how we say something.

And that's when perhaps we remind ourselves or each other of what we learned during the separation. Or one of us is gracious enough, with God's prompting through the Spirit, to be the first to say sorry. It *is* getting easier, comparatively, as it wasn't at all easy to begin with. I'm often reminded of how I felt as I ran down the stairs to welcome the prodigal home, placing my hands over his shoulders and onto his back, just as Rembrandt has the Father doing. It was the outward symbol of the inward thought: forgiving and welcoming and extending grace.

Grace is a gift. As God has extended grace to me, how can I *not* extend grace to others, when he has shown me what true grace looks like? And so my daily prayer has become: 'God, help me to be kind to everyone I meet today, for everyone I meet is carrying a burden I know nothing about.' And for my nearest and dearest, I pray: 'God, help me to show grace and also love upon love, even when I don't feel like it.'

Even when I don't feel like it, I can still show love – even though it sounds prescriptive. Yet without a shadow of doubt it works: four times a day, to hug for at least twenty seconds. A real proper hug. On rising from bed, on returning to bed; on leaving the house and on entering the house. Four times a day, a proper wrap-around hug. Scientists say hugging increases the oxytocin levels in the brain, which lowers stress levels and leads to contentment. It also stimulates dopamine and serotonin levels necessary for pleasure and for guarding against depression. We began to do it by rote and discovered that the prescription works. The feelings follow the action, not the other way around. What begins as cold and prescriptive becomes natural, affirmative and loving.

Our path of forgiveness and rebuilding is a long one. Sometimes it's rocky, and sometimes there are flowers along the way. Sometimes it's steep and demanding, and sometimes it's a stroll on a sunny day. We have determined to walk it together, come what may, because marriage and love are gifts not to be tossed lightly aside but to nurture and work on together.

Kim's reflections

Forgiveness is indeed a journey with twists and turns and setbacks, and it is also a two-way street. We all know that it takes two to tango but the balance of responsibility is rarely 50:50. As the prodigal in this story, I needed to acknowledge my bad decisions and my responsibility for them and to ask for forgiveness. The original granting of that forgiveness and the restoration that followed was a wonderful thing, but whereas God can forgive and forget, we are not so good at the second part.

In my experience, this has taken two forms in the course of our journey. First, I have wondered on occasion whether forgiveness has truly been granted. This is normally a result of my reading too much into a more general reaction to life and circumstances, assuming that hurts have been remembered, when they probably aren't the cause. Second, I often struggle with the common complaint of finding it hard to forgive myself. It has also been helpful to me when Penelope has acknowledged her part, either in the original issues or in the ongoing outworking.

We were a work in progress before this, and we still are! I'm grateful for grace being extended and for the opportunity of the second chance that forgiveness affords. So, the journey continues. It still takes two to tango and, as Penelope says, it's best taken a day at a time in simple but important steps.

Penelope has written about their journey of forgiveness, which included a physical journey walking across rural France, in her book Walking Back to Happiness *(Sarah Grace Publishing, 2019).*

The daily choices

We have both shared how we learned to forgive the other in order to move forward in our marriage. However, while we have dealt with one of the biggest crises in our marriage, over the years we have learned that we need to continue to walk in grace and forgiveness – they are both daily choices. We have come to understand that forgiveness is absolutely vital for a healthy marriage, because, 'Love cannot last long or live out its eternal purpose in human relationships without a foundation of forgiveness.'[3]

There will be many big and little grievances that we experience, and it takes time to learn which need to be addressed and which can be overlooked.[4] For instance, when we have learned some of the more tedious habits our partner has, we can either build them up in our minds until we simply *have* to confront them, or we can take the time to think about whether we can extend grace and forgive them for winding us up (and exercise patience and kindness). If we decide that, in fact, this is a big issue for us, we need to ensure we pick the right moment and have the right attitude to talk to them about it.

Claire: More often than not, when I have asked God whether to confront Steve on a habit, God has replied that I should extend grace, let go of the grievance I feel and show Steve I love him by picking up after him (you can guess what winds me up now!). This does reflect the wisdom of Proverbs: 'Whoever would foster love covers over an offence, but whoever repeats the matter separates close friends' (17:9). Sometimes I have to really consider: is it something I really need to confront or can I cover it over with love, grace and forgiveness?

> Is it something I really need to confront or can I cover it over with love, grace and forgiveness?

But what about those times when our partner says or does something (whether intentionally or not) that really wounds us, when it wouldn't be right to simply pretend we aren't hurting? We can't make our partner behave in a certain way – but how we respond is our responsibility. There may be moments where we have to consciously remove ourselves from the situation in order to calm down and prepare our hearts to explain graciously what has upset us. We may then have to learn to let go and forgive, however much in the right we may feel we are, or however much we have the right to be angry and hurt. Because, ultimately, by hanging on to unforgiveness we are causing bitterness to spring up in our hearts and this will affect not only us but our marriage too.

It may be that we need to explain to our partner how they have hurt us, to give them the opportunity to understand and learn from it. However, we do need to ensure we are speaking graciously rather than out of our hurt (we look in more detail at how to do this sensitively in Chapter 7). As Colossians 3:13 says: 'Bear with each other and forgive one another if any of you has a grievance against someone. Forgive as the Lord forgave you.'

We can be dogged by some of the emotions that stem right back to the beginning of our marriage when our partner offended us in a particular way. The hurt we felt then can feel just as intense in the current moment, and it is easy to bring all of that old baggage back up. We have to remind ourselves that we have chosen to forgive our partner for those things, and God has also forgiven them, so we actually don't have the right to do that – if we did we would then be sinning. It can be hard in the heat of the emotion to remind ourselves of this, but it is the truth. We need to choose again to extend the forgiveness that we chose back then, because forgiveness is the only way we can move forward.

That doesn't mean that we can't express to our partner what we are struggling with – we simply need to ensure we speak out our explanation using our words wisely and graciously. It may be that either one or both of us needs to watch the way that we say or do something because of what it triggers in the other person – it is important to communicate that well, as we are both imperfect people needing grace as we navigate this life. But, unless the person is doing it maliciously, knowing full well the reaction they will cause in the other, it is not a sin that they need to be challenged on. As Paul says, love 'keeps no record of wrongs' (1 Cor. 13:5). While we need to deal with negative emotions if and when they bubble up, we should never consciously keep a bank of all our partner's past mistakes in order to bring them up during arguments (we do know how easy it is to fall into this trap). We can consciously choose not to remember and dwell on them, just as God has with our mistakes: 'I will forgive their wickedness and will remember their sins no more' (Heb. 8:12).

We have looked at the importance of forgiving our spouse and the need to learn how to forgive ourselves. But what about when someone else hurts one or both of us? Sometimes it is easier to forgive someone who has hurt us personally than it is to forgive someone who we know has deeply hurt our spouse.

One piece of advice I was given when I became a pastor's wife was to guard my heart. I was warned that everyone would have an opinion on what my husband was doing, and the decisions he would make, and that, while he might take it in his stride, I would probably find some of it incredibly hurtful as I was offended on his behalf. In the same way, Steve was given advice to guard me as his wife, as people sometimes expect a pastor's wife to behave and function in a predefined way, but I have my own character and set of gifts that may not fit people's expectations. What wise advice! We can become hugely defensive of our partners. We have learned, over time, that the more we continue to walk the path of forgiveness and refuse to take offence at what people say, the less able resentment and bitterness are to find a foothold.

If we keep remembering that, ultimately, we have died to ourselves (and dead people can't get offended) and are living for Christ (see Rom. 6), then that will help us to take our hurts directly to the cross to allow God to help us deal with the pain and show us, always, that there is purpose and hope in our journey.

Over to you

- Are there any issues in your marriage that you can recognize have been left unresolved? Do you need to extend forgiveness to your partner?
- Have you ever thought about self-forgiveness? Can you recognize when you have been too hard on yourself?
- What daily choices can you make to ensure forgiveness is a hallmark of your marriage?

5

Grace Seeks to Understand

Trust in the LORD with all your heart and lean not on your own understanding.

Proverbs 3:5

We are all different, so each one of us will have come to our marriage with our own set of expectations and ideas. Good marriage preparation will have taught us how to manage expectations – and explain that we have to keep revisiting them and keep being honest. As we have said, we never did marriage preparation and Claire, in particular, entered marriage full of unrealistic ideals, which was not the best start!

Each of us needs to understand and celebrate the differences in our partner. Once the honeymoon period is over and we are learning to live with a person who has different ideas about all sorts of aspects of life, we need to learn to still celebrate who they are, rather than trying to change them to be more like we are. In his book *Sacred Marriage*, Gary Thomas reminds us that marriage stops us from being selfish, as we learn how to love all the traits of the person we have chosen to be with – even those traits that seem so mismatched to ours.[1]

There may be times when we simply get overwhelmed with exasperation and wonder whether God made a huge mistake bringing us together, but it is precisely because we are so different that God can use our marriages to transform us. Unfortunately, that is a message we don't hear often – or don't remind ourselves of often enough. For us, the differences between us created a huge degree of separation because we never took (or had) the time to understand.

Claire: I am a very emotional person and can experience low moods that, at times, I can't really explain. Steve isn't so in touch with his emotions, and so when I was feeling emotionally low he really didn't know how to reach out to me. This ended up getting him down – the things he hadn't experienced became a barrier between us as we allowed frustration and fear to take hold.

One of the aspects of Steve's character that I used to find completely alien was his spontaneity. I like to plan everything precisely. Even on holiday, I used to make a list of what we would do each day, and wanted to stick rigidly to it. However, while, over time, Steve has come to appreciate my organizational skills, I have also learned to understand and value his spontaneity. As our lives have got busier, and my capacity slightly less, I have come to look forward to those times when we simply down tools and go and do something spontaneously. And I very rarely plan what we are going to do on holiday before we get there now. Waking up on holiday on some days not having plans has actually become a huge joy, which I never expected.

Steve: As Claire said, my emotional graph would look more like a flat line! My moods rarely change from one day to the next. So I did find navigating this alien landscape of mood swings really challenging. Firstly, I had to learn that Claire's low moods had very little to do with me, and that I should stop taking them personally and reacting defensively. Secondly, I also learned how little I understood about my own emotional state. I realized that for years I had believed that because emotions are unreliable they should be ignored. Maybe it was that oh so British stiff upper lip, or maybe I had learned it as a protective mechanism growing up. Either way, this had led me to neglect my own emotional state. Seeking to understand Claire better has in fact helped me to understand myself better – while I may be less externally emotional, my emotions still matter and I need to listen to what they are telling me.

Embracing and growing through difference

Chine and Mark McDonald come from very different cultural backgrounds, so had to learn to accept and celebrate one another's differences when they came together. As Chine explains below, this was not always easy.

On our anniversary every year, we normally get away for a romantic break and love to reminisce by making time to re-watch our wedding video. It never fails to make both of us cry, as we remember that special day in which our lives changed forever. During Mark's speech, he talked about the similarities in the values both of us hold as important – how each of us strives to make the world a better place. We are both passionate advocates for justice and in different ways have dedicated our lives to just that – Mark through his work with children living in poverty, from difficult family backgrounds and who face all manner of obstacles, and me through my work in international development.

But, in so many ways, we are completely different. I was born in Nigeria and moved to the UK with my parents and two younger sisters when I was 4 years old. Our family moved around the home counties of south-east England a lot, as my parents continued their climb up the career ladder in their professions. Mark was born at home in a coastal town in East Yorkshire and lived there until his mid-twenties, when he moved down to London for work. My family is typically Nigerian. We are loud and proud. We love to sing and dance and get in each other's business. Food is central to our family gatherings; there's usually a lot of it and it contains spice that can blow your head off. Mark's family has the sarcasm, wit and reserved nature of many British families. They're a classic 'meat and two veg' kind of family. When they get together, they talk about big, intellectual things going on in the world. They show their love for each other in a completely different way to how my family does.

Noticing the differences

Mark and I met shortly after we both turned 30. We had both got used to living busy and fulfilling lives as single people, but each hoped we would eventually meet 'The One'. We met initially at a mutual friend's Christmas party. Mark was dressed in a Christmas jumper and I was dressed up as Mrs Claus. In the months that followed, we fell completely and utterly in love. There was so much we had in common. We loved literature and talking about theology and philosophy and politics. We enjoyed getting out and about in London, seeing the latest exhibitions and eating some wonderful meals in lovely restaurants.

Our wedding was the starkest illustration of our two worlds coming together. We made the decision to have two very different celebrations. The first was an elaborate and colourful traditional Nigerian celebration, as we condensed the months-long engagement process of the 'wine carrying' into one day at my parents' house in Hampshire. Around 200 of our friends and family gathered for the occasion, which saw a mere five outfit changes for me and three for Mark. It was loud and raucous and wonderful, and Mark and I had had to get familiar with some traditions that even I never knew existed, including Mark having to buy a long list of very specific gifts for my family members in Nigeria. Three days later, we had our 'traditional white wedding' in a rural church in Surrey, joined by another 250 of our nearest and dearest. While we loved both celebrations and the opportunity to celebrate the duality of my Nigerian heritage and Britishness, Mark sometimes understandably found it overwhelming, but embraced his new family and our new ways with open arms.

While we were dating, we often talked about the fact that we were an inter-racial relationship. Race was something I had thought about and considered daily for most of my life, whereas as a white man, Mark had rarely had to think about it at all. Living in London, we were hardly a rarity, but we often noticed the second looks we got when visiting Bridlington, where Mark is from and where the vast majority of people are white. Mark soon became aware of how different life is for black people in majority white cultures – the things we have to think about that he had never experienced before. The issues of race were brought into sharp focus when we had our son. He is of course bi-racial – something neither Mark or I have experience of being. We recognize the unique challenges, issues and also wonderful and amazing things that he will experience as he grows older.

Growing together
In growing together, we have learned to listen to each other – not just to listen but to really hear and try and understand. Sometimes the differences in our cultural heritage and background make

our experiences and expectations different from each other's. My family expect to be involved in every area of our lives, while Mark's provide a bit more space. There are also all sorts of subtle cultural things that are or are not permissible in Nigerian families. They can be as little as making sure you greet your elders first in the morning, or not saying no to food when visiting someone's house. Sometimes not knowing these things can cause moments of hurt or misunderstanding, but over the years we've learned to understand the subtleties of cultural difference. But there are also differences in our personality types. I am a planner, while Mark is not; Mark is much more spatially aware and practical than I am; I tire myself out by getting involved in too many things, while Mark is rightly selective about when and with whom he spends his time and energy. In learning about our differences, we have grown and understood a little bit more about each other. In that, we have grown to be better versions of ourselves.

Soon after we got married, we found an amazing church that we both loved. I had grown up in church, but, while Mark's late mother was a Methodist minister, it had been a long time since he was engaged in church. In the early days of our relationship, we talked a lot about our differences – theologically, personality-wise and culturally. But we're so thankful that we found a church where all of that could be worked out practically within a loving community in which each of us, and our family, could thrive.

It's an important reminder that not just in marriage but also in the family of God, people of different backgrounds and personalities and hopes and dreams can be reconciled.

Learning to communicate well

Claire: We are often drawn to someone who is very different to ourselves and those differences may well include the way we communicate. It might be that one of you wears your heart on your sleeve and is very open about everything, while the other isn't that sure of how they feel and certainly doesn't know how to communicate any of that (which is what we are like). For many years, we simply didn't have the opportunity to communicate anyway, as Steve wasn't around, and when he was, he struggled to function because he was so exhausted. So it was quite a long way into our marriage that we started to focus on learning to communicate together well. One thing we learned, after some frustrating moments of one of us second-guessing the other: if you don't understand fully what the other person is saying don't try and work it out or assume you will be able to at some point – ask for clarification.

The secret to good communication is . . . listening. As it says in James 1:19: 'everyone should be quick to listen, slow to speak and slow to become angry'. It is as we listen that we learn more about the other person and are able to understand them better. Listening is not just about what we hear, but also learning to observe what is not being said – the non-verbal messages that are being conveyed through body language, facial expressions and even the tone of voice our partner is using.

> It is as we listen that we learn more about the other person and are able to understand them better.

As we listen, we should also learn to empathize – to try and understand what it is like to walk in our partner's shoes. They may, for example, be worked up about something that happened at work, which we consider trivial. If we take the time to listen and understand what the day was like for them, and why they were upset by what happened, we can begin to empathize. We can show them we have been listening by reflecting back some of the phrases they have used. Asking questions to get clarification is helpful too, as it shows our partner that we are keen to understand. Summarizing at the end can give them a real sense that we have listened right the way through to what they have said too. We have learned never to say, 'You shouldn't feel like that.' Feelings are a reality, and while our feelings may be lying to us, our partner should lovingly stand beside us while we work that out rather than lecturing us about our emotions (see Chapter 6).

Love languages

One of the ways that we learned to understand and appreciate the differences between us was through teaching on the 'Five Love Languages'; this was a revelation to us. It was a little while into the new phase in our marriage that we came across *The Marriage Book* by Nicky and Sila Lee.[2] Within that, they mention the 'Five Love Languages' (Gary Chapman has written a book with that title). We had taken to going on walks, pausing to read a chapter of the book together and then discuss it as we continued to walk. Well, we were stopped in our tracks when we got to the mention of the love languages, as it seemed to make so much sense to us; we wondered why we had never heard about them before! As we read on, we learned more about the way our partner likes to receive love – and why we so often miss the mark by offering love in the way that we want to receive it.

The five love languages are: acts of service, gifts, physical touch, time and words of affirmation. When I read about them I immediately knew which mine were (acts of service – and sometimes time). It was also easy to guess Steve's (physical touch and words of affirmation). But it also made me groan – because we don't share the same languages at all! This, we read, is quite usual because, as we all know, opposites attract. But it makes it very difficult to give love in the way the other person wants to receive it, because it does seem like a foreign language to us.

It was really helpful to understand what a different place we are both coming from, trying to express love but doing it in such different ways. For example, I can do lots of things *for* Steve but it doesn't mean anything unless I affirm him vocally. Whereas Steve can tell me until he's blue in the face that he loves me, but if he doesn't back that up with actions then it all just seems like meaningless words to me.

Steve: So how do we make this work, so that we stop missing the mark of being able to reach each other with love? Well, it is down to understanding the other's love language (and the fact that it can change over time – for instance, gifts have gone up on Claire's list. Maybe her tastes have got more expensive, or maybe it is because we don't have to penny pinch quite so much these days, but she has definitely become more relaxed and able to receive gifts as an expression of love). I also know Claire has worked hard at speaking out positive words even though at times I know she must find it cringe-worthy as it can seem overly gushy to her. Yet she is prepared to swallow her pride and embarrassment to communicate her love in a way I can actually understand. As a natural writer, she often finds it easier to write encouraging notes and cards to me (and the kids). It reminds me of the time when we were long-distance dating and would send daily cards to one another (I had a helping hand here as I worked for a card company at the time!). This means that I now have a stack of notes and cards of Claire expressing her love to me over the years in ways that really encourage and affirm our love.

Why do we find it so hard to offer love in the way that our partner enjoys receiving it? As we have said, they usually have the opposite love languages to us. I think our own upbringing has a huge impact on the way we have learned to behave. For instance, perhaps you were taught by your parents to be humble, and so withholding affirmation is sometimes an unconscious way of helping others to be humble too. We can find, culturally, that praise is limited in our nation – as British people we seem to find sarcasm easier than praise (although we know that is something of a sweeping generalization).

Sometimes we can assume our partner must know they are good at something, so there is no point in telling them so. Interestingly, R.T. Kendall includes an anecdote in his book *Your Words Have Power*,[3] about the fact that he still needs affirming each time he preaches – and he experienced first-hand the fact that the great preacher Martyn Lloyd-Jones needed it too! If people so known as being great in their field need it, how much more do we in our everyday lives?

At times, we need to be honest and recognize that we can get totally self-absorbed, particularly if we have a lot on at work or in our family. We get focused on the situations that are causing us stress and so don't recognize when our partner is crying out for some attention. We can ask God daily to help us press the pause button on our lives, not just to receive the peace and wisdom for our current needs but also so we can recognize what is going on in our partner's life too. That's why having regular 'checking in' moments with each other is so important.

Learning to stay connected

Claire: There can be times when I'm at the end of myself – juggling work, looking after our kids, and my roles within church can totally wring out me out to the point that I feel I have little left to give. I know as a busy pastor Steve can often feel wrung out by the end of a day too.

And yet it is so important to keep fighting for those moments of connection. We can work hard both separately and together. In those seasons when we are both focused on very different things, it can almost feel like we are like ships that pass in the

> It is so important to keep fighting for those moments of connection.

night – roomies at best; strangers in the worst moments. But if we just stop for a little while and check in with one another we both instantly feel like we are working towards a common goal and can support and understand where the other one is at. Somehow it lifts what can be a time of struggle, as we realize afresh that we are not alone.

It may well be the case that one of you is more in tune relationally and emotionally, and so has more of an idea of where your marriage is at. As Steve has already indicated, even though I had tried to communicate in the past in my outbursts, because for the majority of the time I had simply put my head down and got on with life, he hadn't fully appreciated the extent of my deep sadness and loneliness. My response was to be incredulous – how could he not know? That's simply not an excuse. No . . . but the more marriage books I've read, the more I've come to understand that it is often the case that one partner has more of a handle on where the relationship is at. And so that person can be the one that reminds both partners that an honest look at the state of the marriage needs to be a regular discussion point. One tool that can help aid such discussion is an annual 'MOT', which is something we suggest to the couples we do pre-marital and marital counselling with. As a couple you can write your own questions, but we suggest you take time out to revisit your vision statement, check you feel on track with one another still and acknowledge where you are doing well (in order to celebrate) as well as recognize, honestly, where you need to make more of an effort with one another.

It can sometimes feel easier to simply not talk, to push difficulties down, as there is so much to cope with in a day already, but when we don't communicate with one another we feel less connected and those painful areas in our lives are allowed to fester rather than get dealt with. Author Sarah Walton spoke to me about how she had to learn to open up more – and how God has worked in both her and her husband to help them communicate more clearly (we hear more from them both in Chapter 9):

> When we don't communicate with one another we feel less connected.

> We had to fight the temptation to shut each other out of, and not be honest about, what we were struggling with or how we were feeling hurt or misunderstood. We needed to be able to listen to each other without trying to fix each other. As we grew in that, we began to grow closer to each other, trusting that we could be open with each other about our struggles, temptations, hurts and grief, and be received with grace and compassion – even if the other couldn't fully understand or fix it. Obviously, we don't always do this well. We're still too quick to speak and too slow to listen at times, and sometimes we retreat away from each other, rather than doing the hard work of being open. However, we are quicker to bring ourselves to Christ when we're wrestling with deep emotions, which in turn, gradually softens our hearts to open up to each other and see the gift that God has given us in having each other to walk through our suffering together.

Unfortunately, I'm a slow learner and I still find myself holding things inside for far longer than I should. But by God's grace, he's grown Jeff to be more proactive in asking me questions and he's grown me in recognizing when I'm stuffing my emotions and internal struggles, and being quicker to open up to Jeff on a more consistent basis. Usually, the longer we hold things inside, the more complicated they become and the harder it becomes to let them out. Therefore, we try to consistently talk through where our hearts are at and where we're struggling, which helps us address issues in a less complicated way. Often, simply bringing them into the open sheds light and truth into the dark areas of our hearts and guards us from the enemy taking advantage of the situation.

If we get into the habit of expressing our feelings and struggles to one another, there is another frustration that can arise: when we expect that our partner should be able to understand how we are feeling and thinking by now, and yet that is not the case. Often that can be because they are wired so differently to us, but also external circumstances and even simply tiredness can create obstacles in our communication; we need to be aware of when that happens.

It is important that we keep extending grace to one another: perhaps you are the one who is getting frustrated, feeling like you are having to keep on sharing as your partner doesn't seem to hear you. Or maybe you find self-examination and expression tiring, and so this level of communication is difficult for you. It is important for us all to be honest about where we stand, but also find the balance to help and support one another so each person feels validated and heard.

Our sense of connection can also be at risk when we face unexpected difficulties and painful losses. We will be looking at these in more detail later, but it is important to acknowledge that we may each respond to hard times in very different ways and that can make us feel isolated from one another. We need to be extra patient with each other, but also make the decision to fight for understanding, even when it seems too hard to achieve. A friend of ours shared openly and honestly with us about how losing a pregnancy very early on ended up causing conflict between her and her husband. She was thrust into deep grief, while he considered it to be a pregnancy that never really happened. They couldn't understand one another's response and so a gulf opened up between them. She ended up pursuing counselling to help her through her grief. The counsellor suggested that they name the baby together and create a box of anything they had already bought for the baby in order to then pray and commit the whole situation to God. The husband agreed to do that in order to help his wife heal, and afterwards they found that they could both move forward, together.

Such loss is devastating and inevitably has an effect on the marriage relationship. As Zoe Clark-Coates, author and CEO of the grief and support charity The Mariposa Trust (more widely known by its primary support division Saying Goodbye)[4] explained to us: 'Some people find loss brings them emotionally closer to their partners; for others, it can put a strain on their relationship.' In order to ensure you stay united, whatever you face, Zoe's advice is invaluable: 'Communication is vital. It is imperative that you both talk about how you feel, and just as importantly listen to one another. Often couples grieve at varying rates and can be at different stages in the grief cycle, and if this isn't discussed and understood, it can cause real conflict. So keep talking. If communication is a problem, consider sitting down with a counsellor, as having a third party help lead the conversation can really help.'

As we have shown, communication is vital in both the everyday but also those particularly fraught and painful times. Taking the time to understand one another – the opinions and expectations you bring from your different backgrounds, how you process events and emotions and how you like to be shown love – will help you support one another well in the long term.

Over to you

- Take some time to look at the love languages and think about which ones are your primary ones, and which you think are your partner's. Then get together and compare lists – did you both agree? (You can find out more about the five love languages, and even take a couple's quiz, at https://www.5lovelanguages.com.) If you have done this previously, it is worth doing again, as your primary languages can change over time.

- Discuss together whether you find it easy or difficult to talk about how you feel. Is one of you usually more in tune with where you are at in your relationship? If you both (or one in particular) find it hard to discuss your feelings, how can you encourage one another in this? (You may like to decide together whether creating MOT questions that you will take time out to work through each year will be helpful for you.)

- Individually, set a challenge for yourself to show love to your partner in the love language that you know they appreciate, but is the one you find hardest.

Grace Gives Space

'There is a time for everything . . . a time to weep and a time to laugh, a time to mourn and a time to dance . . . a time to be silent and a time to speak'.

Ecclesiastes 3:1–7

Learning when to give the other space to process – especially when you are different types of people or when your partner is not in the same place as you emotionally – is vital. This is particularly important when it comes to the different ways we process pain, grief and trauma. We all face each of these things at various times throughout our lives, but the Covid-19 pandemic caused us all to experience difficult emotions – some simply due to being in close proximity to our partners in a way we aren't normally, which made finding space much more challenging. The repercussion of this time of worldwide loss and grief will no doubt be felt for years to come, and the trauma faced by families and keyworkers will affect individuals in a way we don't yet fully comprehend.

Talking with a friend who is a nurse at the start of the second national lockdown in England, we discovered that many medical professionals were signed off work with PTSD. Just imagine the ongoing impact that will have already had on them as individuals, their marriages and families. If you are one of those couples who are navigating this situation right now, we pray that you know God's comfort and healing as you take time to process everything. What a stark reminder that we need to learn how to be gentle with one another, providing support and space to our partners whenever necessary. Later in the chapter you can read how Will and Lucinda Van Der Hart navigated his acute anxiety after he undertook a chaplaincy-type role at a bomb scene on 7/7.

Allowing room for recovery

Steve: I know I have an impatient streak. I want things fixed and I like to be the one to fix them. That's why I love DIY. Show me a leaking pipe or a broken washing machine and I'll be reaching for my tools. Fixing relationship issues is of course never as straightforward. So it was a particularly difficult period for me when Claire needed time away at her parents' as we began rebuilding our marriage. I needed to understand that she needed space – that although I was ready to build afresh, she simply wasn't in that place yet. I had to learn that pressurizing people to make decisions or even simply talk before they are ready, is at best futile and at worst damaging. However much I wanted to know exactly what was going on in her head or how long this 'season' would last, I had to simply allow Claire time to process and heal. This meant being there when she needed to talk (and not offering quick-fix answers of which I had many – mostly unhelpful!) but also being prepared for her not to talk at all.

Claire loves to journal; I had to understand that asking her what she was journaling about was, again, unhelpful. She would later tell me that much of what she was writing was simply stuff she needed to get out of her system rather than statements she truly believed. It would therefore have been hurtful for me to know everything she was thinking and working through. God certainly taught me patience in this time as, even when Claire did decide to come home and start rebuilding our marriage, she still needed space. However, through this time I was learning more about how I need to process hurt too. It actually forced me to reflect on my emotional and mental state rather than rushing on to start building together again. This is something I don't naturally do (again going back to the ignore-it-and-hope-it-will-go-away mode of thought) but something I have learned is vital. I grew up thinking emotions are untrustworthy (which is true) but wrongly concluded they should therefore be ignored. I can see now that it wasn't just Claire that needed the space – I did too. As I was left searching in the silence and trying to understand where she was at, God graciously showed me where I was at instead.

> As I was left searching in the silence and trying to understand where she was at, God graciously showed me where I was at instead.

Still, giving your partner space while they continue to process pain, shame and disappointment can be exhausting. I remember saying to Claire: 'I'm not sure I can keep this up,' as I continued to reach out in love, when everything in me was dying to know what was going on in her head. I was desperate for things to hurry up!

I needed to learn that it wasn't all down to me, and that I could and should be relying on God's grace working in our marriage – it was after all no small miracle that we had been brought back together. I could trust the Holy Spirit to empower, guide and set the pace of our rebuilding as well as cover the mistakes we inevitably made. I had to grow in patience and learn to be still and know that God was God (and I wasn't). However quickly I wanted things to get back on track, I had to trust God's timing and what he was doing . . . in both our hearts.

Claire: I talked earlier about facing regular moments in which I was enveloped afresh by grief, pain and the anguish of rejection after moving back home. While Steve did hold me and reassure me of his love when I felt able to receive that, there were other times when I couldn't do so. I found my journal was incredibly helpful as a way I could pour out all my confused, hurting emotions. Somehow writing them down, then seeing them in black and white, helped me to distinguish between what was simply pure emotion that I was processing and what were lies that I needed to repent of keeping hold of. I spent a lot of time writing down conversations with God – they were very psalm-like in their rawness, but God always interacted with me gently, pouring his grace over me every, single, time.

Steve gave me the opportunity to journal whenever I needed to – and, in moments of intense pain, still does. I can remember a family holiday, staying in a cottage with both of our kids. I was working through the pain of letting go of past lies and longings, as well as continuing to process how postnatal depression made me feel on a day-to-day basis. He graciously gave me the time to journal, utilizing the wonderful green space just outside the lovely New Forest holiday cottage to play with the children so that I could have some quiet time to myself.

I also found I needed time with a counsellor individually, and had to travel for that. As I didn't drive at the time (and would have hated driving there even if I did), Steve always took me to the counselling sessions, simply waiting outside for me. While he may have asked me whether I found a session helpful, he never pried or pushed me for information (I for one would have been eager to know what progress was being made). His patience and generosity of time are things I have enjoyed and benefited from, but not always recognized.

Space to grieve

More recently, as I experienced unexpected floods of tears, I recognized that I was grieving my dear mum even before she died. We were told she wasn't going to live past Christmas . . . three years running. Seeing someone who has had such a tremendous impact on your life and faith, and who you love so much, slowly fade away while coping with an incredible amount of pain and suffering, is intensely difficult.

I didn't feel the strain keenly at first, but my body certainly did – and the unexpected tears became a more regular outlet for me. There were tiny triggers that would set me off, and I would find myself crying at the TV and at things I read in books or online. In fact, that is quite common now, and sometimes I need to hide away and process how I'm feeling before I can even express anything verbally. Steve is kind enough to recognize this and facilitates that. He also takes time to explain what is going on to our kids when I find myself totally overwhelmed.

I used to feel guilty when I cried in front of our children – until we had the conversation about whether they wanted to be there when their Grandma died and they said they did. I realized then that sheltering them from deeply intense grief would make it harder, not easier, for them to process their own when the time came (and that it was good for them to learn how to accommodate and make space for someone who is dealing with difficult emotions).

They respond to my involuntary tears differently: our son usually just makes a flippant comment like, 'Oh mum is crying – again,' whereas our daughter is more empathetic and wants to know whether I will be alright. But I've decided it is important for them to see what grief looks like – too often, we sanitize various aspects of life today and it is to our detriment, as we have no room to process well. Watching a loved one die is one of the most intensely difficult experiences we will probably all face, and yet our culture likes to cover up death, so we have no idea of what it will be like beforehand.

Steve has also driven us down to see my family every single school holiday for the past three or four years (as we have been supporting other family members through difficulties too). It hasn't been easy for any of us, but both he and the kids have understood the need for me to be there for those I am close to, and have, for the most part, facilitated that without grumbling.

Occasionally I took a few days to visit my sister and parents, and Steve took over the roles that I usually do to ensure that I could go (he does that during weekends when I am speaking somewhere too – it is part of us giving one another space for what we need to engage with at the time, which we look at more closely in Chapter 9).

When I am back home, there are times when Steve asks me how I am and I simply don't know. I don't have the words, or the understanding of where I'm at, to express verbally what is going on inside. Now mum has died, I'm dealing with the overwhelming waves of darkness that grief can suddenly engulf you with, when you least expect it. He understands that and doesn't push me – he waits for me to share or lets it go if he can tell I'm not in a place to share quite yet. Often I find I need space just to be before God, or need the opportunity to sit and pour out how I'm feeling through writing in a file I've created purely for that purpose. At other times, as soon as we finish a visit to my family I am itching to speak to him, simply waiting until we get home if what I need to say isn't appropriate for our children to hear.

At times it may seem to the partner not grieving that they are walking on eggshells, but it is so important that the person who *is* grieving knows that they are loved and being cared for. Taking the time to share where you are at in your grief journey is important, although difficult at times. And in those moments when you simply don't know, your partner can be asking the Holy Spirit for guidance about when to step back and give you space, and when to suggest you spend time together. As Zoe Clark-Coates, grief expert, explained to me: 'This may mean just sitting in the same space watching Netflix, or it could be going for a walk. Grief can make people feel isolated and alone, so it is essential to consciously make the time to be with one another.' Getting the balance right between space alone and space together may be tricky at times, but being gentle, considerate and patient with one another helps you to stay connected in what is a very painful time.

Grace for the waiting

Learning when to give the other space is quite an art; I'm not sure I've got it quite right, especially as Steve often needs a gentle prompt to start thinking about where he is at emotionally.

Our partners will face some of the same situations as we do, but will often respond to them completely differently. They will need the opportunity to respond in the way that is best for them, which can, sometimes, be frustrating for us if we are going through the same thing and want to talk and pray about it but they aren't quite ready. Maybe one of you is an external processor while the other processes everything internally – that means you may be ready to talk something out straight away, and you will need to fight against the frustration that threatens to boil over when you have to wait patiently, giving your spouse time to think through an issue before discussing it with you.

Our partners will also have many other situations that they face that are unique to them. They often spend their days in a different place to us – and obviously come from a different family. Your spouse may be facing challenges that you are not, and yet it still affects you deeply. For example, if your partner struggles with their mental health, for whatever reason, that will require you to give them ongoing grace and space, however painful it is for you (and please know I understand that can be *intensely* painful). It will also require deep understanding and godly wisdom, and it may be that you need support yourself in order to be a support to your partner, or recognize that you need to make changes to your own behaviour (see Glen and Emma's piece in Chapter 8).

God's greatest work is often in the waiting – in the times when you are looking on hopelessly, watching your partner struggle, offering the help you can but also realizing that, ultimately, you are powerless to change the situation. When you, and your partner, understand that it is only God who can make a difference, and he may or may not choose to step in and change things, how you respond to that will determine not

Grace-Filled Marriage

When you are waiting for him to do a work in your partner, he is, ironically, probably doing more work in your heart.

only the depth of your relationship with him, but also with your husband or wife. As Steve learned in our early days back together (and we are both still learning today) God's deepest work is often done in those moments of waiting, when you are waiting for him to do a work in your partner, he is, ironically, probably doing more work in your heart.

Space to process

To go right back to the beginning of our marriage, I also want to tackle the thorny subject of our sex life, because it was not straightforward at all, and it is another area that Steve has shown such patience and loving care in. I had had a word spoken over me by someone in my teenage years that had caused a deep-seated fear of sex and so, while I felt very passionately towards Steve, there was only so far I could go physically without completely clamming up. With Steve so often working around the clock, you can imagine how our sex life fared in the early years. With little time for each other, and being exhausted when we did see one another, we didn't have the opportunity or the physical capacity to work on this side of our marriage. It took quite a few years for us to feel that we could simply make love whenever we wanted to without it taking a huge emotional effort to do so. But, even though there was a whole period when Steve was physically wrung out and so all aspects of our marriage seemed to be on hold, he had actually learned right from the start to walk patiently and carefully with me, showing me how much he cherished time with me whatever happened or didn't happen. The loving environment he cultivated helped me to walk free of those damaging words. In that time, we learned the importance of physical intimacy in marriage, but we also learned it was never to become an idol that we worshipped over and above God. While it seemed unreachable at times, God showed us how we could still visibly demonstrate our love and desire for one another. We also learned that sex is not for our own individual benefit, which is the message we can so easily pick up from culture (see Chapter 9 for Jeff and Sarah Walton's story, which demonstrates this lesson so beautifully). Both of us, in very different ways, learned the importance of the sacrificial giving of ourselves to and for the other.

Giving one another space truly is an act of selfless love

Will and Lucinda Van der Hart never expected that one of them would face a mental health crisis. Navigating this early on in their marriage meant that they had to learn to understand what each of them was going through, give one another space when necessary and, ultimately, work together to strengthen their relationship.

Will: However much we might know that we are loved without condition, very few people actually enter marriage believing it fully, let alone living it confidently. Indeed, the full realization of being unconditionally loved is not made in every marriage, and those who are blessed by its appearance may be staggering out of an experience of dark disempowerment. This was our experience.

We married at university where I was a postgraduate student and Lucinda was an undergraduate. Despite both being young, I quickly adopted a role in the relationship of being the 'secure and dependable' partner. Looking back, I can see how, despite Lucinda loving me without condition, my own insecurity led me to believe that I had to 'be useful'. It wasn't just our relationship that was impacted by this belief, it was work too. I tended to work too hard, do too much and worry that I would let people down. This was the backdrop to what happened on 7 July 2005.

A huge impact

Lucinda was going to a conference in Oxford and I walked her to Paddington Station from our small flat off Edgware Road. On my return at about 9.15 a.m., there was a small gathering of police men and women outside the tube station. There was little indication at that stage that we were in fact facing the largest terrorist incident that the UK had experienced since World War II. Without going into great detail (for that is not what this account is really about), I got deeply involved in the situation by playing a chaplaincy-style role to the emergency services over that first 24 hours. This event turned out to be hugely psychologically impacting to me, far beyond what I might have imagined.

Neither Lucinda nor I had a framework for understanding mental health at that stage, but she could sense that something was deeply troubling me over the summer months. Having been quite an extrovert, I began to spend more time alone. I was more sullen, more irritable and much more anxious. Lucinda knew something was up and tried to give me space to process what I had been through.

The magnitude of what I was experiencing wasn't fully realized until we returned to London to resume work after our summer holidays at the end of August. For me it was a combination of proximity to the tube station, the resumption of work and the return of the student population (whom we were working with). There was also the gnawing sense that I was struggling to be the 'solid and dependable' husband that ensured my 'right to be loved'.

It was actually in the cinema with Lucinda, watching a very sedate costume drama, that I had my first panic attack. After that, the floodgates opened and I was suddenly overwhelmed by a flood of psychological phenomena related to acute anxiety and PTSD. I stopped sleeping properly, lost my appetite and was constantly on edge. For a young couple that had been married for barely two years, the whole situation was completely overwhelming.

Lucinda: Seeing Will physically shaking was so incongruous to me. He had always been so strong and confident, but suddenly he looked fragile and afraid. I knew that I needed to stay calm and be reassuring, but inside I was pretty unsure about how to handle this. At the time mental health was rarely spoken about publicly, and neither of us had read much on the subject. We were both in the dark as to the way forward.

Navigating new territory

One of the great challenges of mental health in marriage is that you just cannot know what your partner is experiencing within. I was totally dependent upon Will's ability to communicate his experiences to me and, even then, I didn't really know what the right response was. Getting him to the doctor was a huge relief. We were blessed to have a very understanding and empathetic GP, who gave Will longer appointments than usual, and really tried to understand what was going on. Finally, I felt that someone professional was supporting us. Alongside that, I simply tried to keep on listening. Will wanted to walk and talk when he was recovering, sometimes for hours. It seemed like a small thing to me, but I could see how important it was for him, and how everyday there was just a little bit of improvement. For a while, every evening after work we went for a long walk together through central London, talking and praying and listening to one another. Reflecting back on the experience, I knew that I couldn't fix Will – only God could do that work. But I could listen patiently and try to give him the time and space he needed to begin to find healing.

Will: The first weekend that I was really unwell was terrible. Lucinda was strong and reassuring but I could tell she was upset and worried about me. This was completely new territory for us, because as well as dealing with the psychological impact of acute anxiety I also felt my 'secure and dependable' persona in our marriage was crumbling. Alongside all of the other rushing thoughts about 7/7, I started to fear being locked away in a psychiatric hospital, with Lucinda on the other side of the glass.

Mental health recovery is not a bell graph, it's a very erratic journey that needs to be measured in weeks and months, not days. At the same time, we saw massive improvements in my symptoms and mood within about six weeks of onset. I was initially diagnosed with an episode of 'acute anxiety', which covered this worst, hellish period. As my acute symptoms faded, I was left with some residual anxiety and persistent worried thoughts, and so my diagnosis was changed to Generalized Anxiety Disorder. That phase lasted for a couple of years.

Embracing unconditional love and equality
Alongside all of these struggles, we were still a young couple trying to build a healthy marriage. What I didn't realize at the time, was that my mental illness was helping us, not hindering us, on that journey. Without glamorizing or simplifying the experience,

or diminishing the pain that we both experienced, there were two specific upsides: my illness positively recalibrated my understanding of unconditional love and it levelled a distorted power balance between us.

Acute anxiety stripped me back to my vulnerable reality and disempowered my ability to work for love. For me, the remarkable, sacrificial and fierce love that Lucinda showed me over that period of our lives blew me away. It was the first time in my life that I had ever felt love without condition. The impact on my life could not have been more significant; it has moved me from being a people pleaser to a people leader.

Secondarily, and more significantly, it gave Lucinda the space to emerge from the shadow of my 'strong and dependable' persona as an equal (or better than equal) partner. I realized that I had been unconsciously patronizing her and assuming more of myself than I should. This realization levelled out our marriage and fostered greater collaboration and mutual respect. We have a range of strengths and weaknesses (that we understand well after seventeen years of marriage), but we don't subscribe to anything less than equality in the way we relate to each other.

A year after my anxiety breakdown we stood on the top of the highest mountain in South East Asia watching the sun rise. It was a setting that I couldn't have imagined eleven months previously, but Lucinda had insisted that we fully embrace life's adventure together. She pretty much pulled me up those 14,000 feet to the top. If anything, it epitomized my mental health recovery, but it also illustrated the new reality of my marriage to this strong, courageous and loving woman.

Will is one of the founding directors of Mind and Soul Foundation, which seeks to educate, equip and encourage the Church in the sphere of mental health: https://www.mindandsoulfoundation.org

Over to you

- Does one of you have a tendency to push for conversation when the other isn't ready? How can you best facilitate that person's need for space while also acknowledging the other's need to talk?
- Discuss together the different ways that you each need space. How can you cultivate those into your daily routines?
- Are either of you (or both) facing some difficult circumstances that mean you need space to process? Discuss together how you can navigate this more unusual time with grace for one another.

7

Grace in Times of Conflict

Everyone should be quick to listen, slow to speak and slow to become angry, because human anger does not produce the righteousness that God desires.

James 1:19–20

Understanding why conflict occurs

Claire: So many of our conflicts can happen because we are feeling stressed, don't feel that our partner is supporting us in the way that they should, or feel that they aren't taking the time to understand why we are feeling the way we are. When I was working with counsellor Chris Ledger on the book *Insight into Managing Conflict* I learned a lot about the reasons behind why we can have the tendency to argue. So much resonated with my own experiences. For example, in that book we look at how our conflicts can arise due to the fact we are placing our hopes in another person – looking to them to meet what are, essentially, spiritual needs, when in reality only God can fulfil them (I mentioned in Chapter 2 that I did that constantly in the early years of marriage). What is interesting is how, when we are then inevitably disappointed by the lack of fulfilment received, we can become critical and judgemental of the other, which, in turn, creates a conflict. That has certainly happened in our marriage in the past.

Our inner belief systems can cause conflict too. For instance, if we have an underlying sense of insecurity and look to our accomplishments to give us a sense of significance, in a conflict we can always feel the need to be in control, which will necessitate pushing the other down. Whereas if we have low self-esteem, we can give in to demands quickly in order to try to be accepted, which means in conflict we aim for peace at any price.

Another point covered in *Managing Conflict* is the need to recognize that Satan will try and disrupt our relationships by purposely stirring up trouble – and we will certainly need to be aware of his schemes. (Now that we are both in ministry, we can definitely sense the atmosphere of our home shifting at times when one or other – or both – of us have an event coming up. Often we can sense him trying to cause conflict to make us feel inadequate for what we are doing.) Having said all that, we also do need to acknowledge that, as humans, we like to get our own way and, when we don't, we can react badly. We can be selfish, arrogant and unrealistic in what we demand from our partner and that can create difficulties in the relationship. As we've seen, we can view all sorts of things from very different viewpoints, and that can cause conflict too. When that affects a deeply held value, one partner can get extremely upset. Often conflict resolution involves trying to work out exactly what it is that has caused the conflict and where both people stand (and whether they are willing to change that stance).

We have certainly seen how different approaches to life can cause conflict in our own relationship. Often it is simply down to a difference in style, but due to the hurt it causes, sometimes we don't see that. It is important to take a step back and realize that we are still on the same page, otherwise it could cause a deeper problem than it needs to. Recognizing that my way isn't the only way has been a big lesson for me. As I highlighted in *Insight into Managing Conflict*, it may be that in a particular situation there isn't a right or wrong, 'but conflict occurs when another won't accept, or validate, the other person's style'.[1] I have come up against this time and time again since we have had children. Steve has a very different approach to me: while we have already discussed our values and know what we want to teach our children, I can feel my anger levels rising when Steve is outworking those principles in a completely different way to the way I would do it. I have to learn to give him space to do that – as long as we are sticking to our agreed values, our children actually benefit from our different approaches, as it gives them a more rounded upbringing.

> Different approaches to life can cause conflict.

Steve: Conflict between us is caused not only by having different viewpoints, but also by our very different responses to conflict. I still find conflict deeply uncomfortable. However, I know it is inevitable, and provides an opportunity for growth. For years, as you have probably gathered, I avoided it at great cost. I can still find myself avoiding it, even now. Claire, on the other hand, likes to deal with things straight away, which often means she speaks out of her feelings and emotions more than simply the issue at hand; whereas I have a tendency to push down how I am feeling to keep things calm. As an internal processor, I like to take things on board and think about my response. There are two dangers with this. The first danger is that I can simply shut down and go

quiet – this has the tendency to infuriate Claire who is needing some kind of indication that I have actually heard her
point of view. The second danger is that in internalizing my
thoughts I can bury them. At some stage the issue needs to be
processed externally and choosing the time to do that is hugely
important.

Some things do require immediate attention, but we need
to be able to listen to where we ourselves are at and ask the
question: will externally processing this issue be fruitful at this
time? And if you are the sort of person who wears their heart
on their sleeve it can be really hard to calm your voice and
communicate with calmness and clarity, but if your partner is
someone who buries their emotions, then they will most likely
shut down and stop listening when volume levels rise. It is
therefore vitally important to understand the way each person
is wired and then give space for one another to voice how they
are feeling without judgement.

Sometimes our partner simply needs to vent – if you normally shut down on these occasions, please try to listen to what
is actually been communicated behind the emotion. And if
your partner is the one who shuts down, please patiently help
them to draw out what is going on inside once they have had
some time to work it through.

That all takes a lot of practise, though (we will look at the
practicalities of when to confront and when to stay silent later
on in this chapter). What we can begin to do straightaway,
however, is learn to be more aware of why we respond to conflict in the way that we do, and what that reveals. It may be
that the anger is locating where a problem lies, which may need
discussing at a later point. We need to take the time to work

that out, though, rather than going straight for the jugular in an argument that may not be necessary.

Claire: Anger is not necessarily sinful – it's what we do with it that matters. As it says in Ephesians 4:26: 'In your anger do not sin'. I have learned a lot from looking at Jesus' example, and was really reassured when I first realized that Jesus felt emotion, deeply – it isn't that our feelings are wrong. While Jesus' response to the money exchangers and those selling animals at the temple is the obvious example of him showing righteous anger (Mark 11:15–17), I often go back to the garden of Gethsemane to remind myself what Jesus did with his negative emotions. In Matthew 26:36–45 we see he was honest with his closest companions about his internal anguish: 'My soul is overwhelmed with sorrow to the point of death' (v.38). We can let our partner know if we are upset about something. But then what did Jesus do? He went to speak to his father: 'Going a little farther, he fell with his face to the ground and prayed, "My Father, if it is possible, may this cup be taken from me. Yet not as I will, but as you will."' (v.39). If we took the time to take our grievances to God, to spill out the raw emotion to him, but then take time in his presence before finally asking him for the grace to act out his will rather than our own, I think conflict resolution within our marriages would be very different.

Checking our heart attitude during times of conflict

I was talking to a friend about all of this, and she told me about being personally challenged when delivering material for a marriage seminar she and her husband were running.

God was getting her to think about taking space and then offering grace too:

> We start the seminar talking about what the foundation for marriage should be:
>
>> According to the grace of God given to me, like a skilled master builder I laid a foundation, and someone else is building upon it. Let each one take care how he builds upon it. For no one can lay a foundation other than that which is laid, which is Jesus Christ.
>> 1 Corinthians 3:10–11, ESV
>
> When we explore what it looks like to build on Jesus, we talk about how it means we build with grace. We use the story of the prodigal son to explain more (Luke 15:11–32). As I read through it, I was really struck by some points afresh: the young man had effectively declared his father dead by asking for his inheritance before time. He had shown gross disrespect to his father's face, and had then gone on to squander the money on rubbish – his father's life's work all gone in a matter of days! After a period of squalid living and hunger, he decided to go home, to beg forgiveness – in all his poverty and pig filth.
>
>> But while he was still a long way off, his father saw him and was filled with compassion for him; he ran to his son, threw his arms round him and kissed him.
>>
>> Luke 15:20
>
> That really is a picture of grace. The son doesn't deserve the father's response but the father literally ran to him, embraced and kissed him.

I was really challenged while talking about it in the seminar. It made me ask myself: do I give grace to Sam when we argue? Often there will be words that cause a rift between us. Normally we take some physical space to recover, and sometimes to stop ourselves saying things we will regret later.

One way or another I will end up in the kitchen, probably cooking the next meal. Sam might then come through the door – what's my response? Do I run to him, feel compassion, embrace and kiss him? More often than not, I am standing still, probably still smarting, waiting for an apology, an explanation, to hear his voice and hear his tone change. That's not grace. That's conditional love. That isn't godly. And it's not building on the right foundation. Grace is giving what isn't deserved, pouring it out unreservedly.

I am still being challenged by this, but I keep asking God for more of his grace in my heart so that I might pour out more in my marriage.

Practical considerations

As we cover in Chapter 8, learning what 'pushes our buttons' is really helpful when we have conflict to resolve. If tiredness causes you to be more confrontational, then leave the discussions to a day when you aren't so tired. If you have had a very difficult day at work, and you know it has caused you to feel more negative generally, ask your partner if you can rearrange when to have your discussion. If you like to have a glass of wine to unwind after a long, hard day, but you know alcohol can make you more aggressive, choose not to drink on a night you know you have things to talk over. In fact, all the usual advice on eating healthily and exercising regularly also impacts the way that we handle conflict too – if our minds and bodies are healthy, it makes it easier for our responses to be too.

Creating the right environment to be able to discuss matters in a calm way is the goal.

I don't always get this right, and can often fall back into my usual way of responding with a flare-up of anger. I was recently reminded of this proverb though, which certainly cuts to the heart of the matter: 'Fools give full vent to their rage, but the wise bring calm in the end' (Prov. 29:11). Creating the right environment to be able to discuss matters in a calm way is the goal, and this can sometimes be as simple as taking some time out while angry, or learning to speak more quietly and gently when you are in your discussion: 'A gentle answer turns away wrath, but a harsh word stirs up anger' (Prov. 15:1). I certainly know how it takes the wind out of my anger sails when Steve refuses to take the bait, but remains calm and gentle. My anger doesn't really have anywhere to go, and so it dissipates as I realize how unnecessary it actually is.

So how should you talk to one another, once you are both calm enough to discuss whatever issue you have conflicting opinions on?

We can still come to the table desperate to get our point of view across, but it is so important to give the other person space to speak, and really take the time to listen (why not offer to allow your partner to go first next time and see what difference that makes?). I read a very pertinent reminder on social media today, in the form of a quote from the Dalai Lama: 'When you talk, you are only repeating what you already know. But if you listen, you may learn something new.' This is very reminiscent of the wisdom found in Proverbs 1:5: 'Let the wise listen and add to their learning'. If we can lay our self-interest aside and take the time to really listen to our partner, we may indeed learn something that changes our opinion on the issue that is at the root of the conflict. We are all prone to faulty thinking, which is why the Bible tells us to: 'be transformed by the renewing of your mind' (Rom. 12:2).

When we are the one speaking, it is important to choose our words carefully. When we speak out of anger, our tone can be one of bitterness, but if we have taken those feelings to God first, hopefully we are able to be more gracious with our explanations. Paul teaches us to speak the truth in love in Ephesians 4:15, and love is certainly a vital component in extending grace to one another. If you are going to be talking over quite a tricky issue, it can help to start with affirmation – something positive – rather than launching into confrontation. Let your partner know that you are keen to work through this because you value your relationship more than the issue.

One of the many helpful nuggets of wisdom that our counsellors taught us was the difference between 'You' and 'I' statements, particularly when we are expressing something we feel strongly about. If we explain why we are upset with the other person by saying: 'You made me feel . . .' we immediately apportion blame, but if we say 'I feel . . .' we take responsibility for how we are feeling. While it may be something that our partner has or hasn't done that is making us feel upset or angry, we need to take responsibility for our own emotions and actions – our response to their actions (there is more on taking responsibility in Chapter 8).

In the same vein, stick to the point. In conflict it can be too easy to launch into: 'You always . . .' or 'You never . . .' making the argument all-encompassing. Don't bring up past grievances (love 'keeps no record of wrongs' – 1 Cor. 13:5) and don't over generalize, as it simply escalates the problem.

Love can help us to ride out disagreements without allowing them to affect our ongoing relationship.

While this can be difficult when we are in the midst of dealing with conflict, it is so important to remember that we are a team who are ultimately both on the same side. Love can help us to ride out disagreements without allowing them to affect our ongoing relationship. As it says in 1 Peter 4:8: 'Above all, love each other deeply, because love covers over a multitude of sins.' While fighting with one another can make this hard to see, what we want to do is work towards a peaceable, sensible, solution. Sometimes this will necessitate letting go of our need to be 'right', learning to apologize when we need to, letting go of any pain we feel has been caused to us and sometimes compromising – in a way that we are both happy with. It may be that a lot of deep hurt has been caused by one or other of you; in that case, it would be wise to ask trusted friends to counsel and pray with you. At the very least, acknowledging the hurt and giving space for the Holy Spirit to bring comfort and healing will help facilitate a sense of togetherness as you seek to resolve the conflict.

It may be that it takes time for the conflict to be resolved: in that period, it is vital to keep asking God for wisdom, to keep extending grace to the other person and to keep humbly asking God 'if there is any offensive way in me' (Ps. 139:24).

Learning when to confront – and when to stay silent

I have to admit that I have always worn my heart on my sleeve. If I am upset or angry, even if I try to hide the fact, my body language and/or facial expressions give my emotions away.

I find it so difficult to leave an issue unresolved and, in the past, used to use the time that Steve was at work to really stew on it further, blowing it up even more in my mind so it became pretty enormous. If only I'd used that time to take my hurt to God in prayer, offer it up to him, ask for him to shine a light on the darkness in my own heart and then look practically at ways to apply his wisdom to whatever was going on. I think our conversations would have been very different . . .

When our marriage counsellors told us that we needed to learn when to bring an issue up and when to save it for another time, I got extremely frustrated. I confront, I work to resolve – and I thought that was good! But they explained that there will be times when it is simply inappropriate to expect to be able to resolve something well. (This is something I didn't fully understand until we had little children, who still needed to be fed, watered and interacted with no matter what issues were going on in their parents' marriage.) The counsellors asked us to write down the things that we knew we found difficult to handle when we are really tired and to then set aside time to talk those things through when we were both ready. One extra piece of advice they gave that I found particularly helpful was when they said that we can give it over to God, for him to look after until we have a chance to go back to it. That's exercising trust again!

We have been looking specifically at conflict, but sometimes we need to have difficult conversations that aren't based on a particular argument, but on the behaviour of one or other of us. Perhaps there is some ongoing sin, or the person has been particularly thoughtless. For those whose default is to avoid confrontation, or to immediately think that it is their fault the other person is behaving as they are, the 'easiest' response is to brush it under the carpet and decide not to deal with it.

But, when we understand that marriage is a means by which God moulds and changes us, it is actually important for us to be honest with one another when a character flaw or certain behaviour needs confronting.

As we have said above, broaching the subject carefully, when we are calm rather than riled by it, is important. Speaking with words of love and grace reflects God's heart. After all, the Bible says: 'the Lord disciplines the one he loves' (Heb. 12:6). We are not saying you have carte blanche to 'discipline' your partner whenever you see fit; rather that the motivation behind speaking up should be love – and a desire to see them walk into greater freedom.

If you are the one who is being spoken to, you may find it really difficult to be on the receiving end of someone pointing out a fault. I can struggle deeply with this, but know the difference when Steve is doing it out of love or anger. When it is loving, I try to be humble and listen well – even if I need to go away and process it with God on my own.

Of course, there may well be times when our partner is finding things really difficult, and so their behaviour reflects that. If this is a one-off, not a pattern of behaviour, then rather than immediately jumping on the behaviour, perhaps we need to take the time to ask God why they are acting the way that they are (if we don't know) and then pray into that. It could be that past hurt has risen to the surface, and they will need gentle coaxing and prayerful support to work through it (see Chapter 8 for more on this). It may be that God shows us we don't need to say anything about the behaviour – what we actually need to do is extend grace and try and alleviate the stress they are feeling currently. Sarah and Jeff Walton, who are dealing with chronic illnesses within their family (which you can read about in Chapter 9), recognize the tension with this, and how suffering can affect behaviour. They have such wisdom to share:

> Suffering doesn't make us sinful; it simply draws our sin to the surface. As much as we can see that as a bad thing, it's God's grace that he allows us to see the true state of our heart in order that we fully grasp the good news of the gospel and allow his Spirit to work in those hidden places of our heart. We have to remember that the same is true for our spouse. It's easy to excuse our own sinful response to suffering, while condemning our spouse's. So, before we react to our spouse, we need to remind ourselves of what Christ has done for us so that we can respond with grace and humility, knowing when to be quiet and let the Spirit work in our spouse and when to gently point out an area of struggle. But if we're willing to point out our spouse's sin, we have to be willing to receive their gentle correction as well. One thing that has helped in regards to when to speak and when to be quiet has been asking ourselves if our spouse is speaking out of emotion (or as Job says, 'speaking words of the wind' [see Job 6:26; 8:2]), which is often spoken out of grief rather than theological belief. We don't need to correct everything our spouse says that isn't true in the heat of the moment, but gently and humbly point out or challenge a consistent action or way of thinking that becomes a pattern. Our aim is to bless our spouse by pointing them to greater freedom in Christ, not burdening them down with harsh and unhelpful words.

I find that so helpful – because we all have times of 'speaking words of the wind' don't we? In fact, it is common to experience heightened emotions and more frequent conflict in times of prolonged stress, and this can cause us to say things that we don't actually mean. We heard from many couples during the lockdown due to Covid-19 who expressed how their relationship was put under extra pressure. That isn't at all surprising, as we were asked to work from home if we were able to. Those personalities who thrive on the social aspect of meeting people in the workplace would have been affected by the isolation. Others may have enjoyed the quiet, but the majority of us felt we were dealing with added stress, as well as confusion and a sense of loss. Combine that altogether, and it is easy to see how couples may have got 'scratchy' with one another. Being able to recognize this is a first step; talking about how we are feeling, but also being kind to one another is so important – at all times, but especially vital in times of heightened difficulty.

Calm instead of conflict

American marriage coach and blogger Tiffany Montgomery shares how God taught her to respond to her husband's mistakes with grace and love, rather than causing conflict.

Eleven months nursing a colicky baby while caring for a toddler stuck in the terrifying threes had me struggling. No one in our house was sleeping. No one in our house was on speaking terms really. A year of colic will do that to a family.

Then, without warning, my husband quit his job.

I was livid, but also afraid. You see we had a plan. Over a year earlier, God called me to quit my well-paid job and stay at home to raise our small children. Bud agreed to take on the financial burden while we stepped out in faith.

Then he went off the plan without so much as mentioning it to me.

That night things exploded. I had carefully crafted a 'dinner talk', with the hopes of opening up communication. With the toddler strapped into her high chair and the baby asleep, we began dinner with a general sense of hostility.

'Bud you have to get a job quickly or we'll miss our mortgage payment.' I volleyed this difficult conversation at him, but was met with silence until dinner ended.

What Bud finally said levelled me.

'Tiffany, I get disrespected at work and I get disrespected at home. I can't deal with it from both places.'

I didn't understand in that moment what he was talking about at all. In desperation, I turned to my pastor's wife – a mentor who came at just the right time and challenged me to seek God instead of divorce.

A painful lesson

Over the weeks to come, God brought a verse to me repeatedly. My mentor would talk to me about prayer and Bible study and God would bring this verse out again and again:

> It is better to live in a desert land
> Than with a contentious and vexing woman.
> Proverbs 21:19, NASB

I did not agree with God, at the time, that I was a contentious woman. Honestly, I was a tired woman. Have you ever noticed that true exhaustion often brings out the real nature we hide behind pretence? God was showing me that the fatigue of the past year had peeled back and exposed layers of pride, arrogance, impatience, selfishness and unforgiveness. My husband was living with all of those things – and they were not part of the plan either.

With prayer and fasting, God began to teach me through the Bible what it means to be a godly wife. My personal examples of marriage came from a legacy of divorce and an appetite for romance novels. What I needed was to understand God's design for marriage.

This sweet mentor encouraged me to stop talking to my husband about things I wanted to change (for a time), as a way to surrender to God's leading and not be 'a contentious and vexing woman'.

No nagging.

No criticism.

No sharing my preference.

I was to pray instead. God began to show me my part in our marriage struggles.

Don't misunderstand me, I am not giving my husband an out for quitting his job. He made an unwise choice that hurt our family. He realized it almost immediately, but the damage was already done. What he needed from his wife was support and understanding while he figured out how to fix things. He got criticism and condemnation instead. When I stopped beating him up over the mistake, things got better and, eventually, he went back to work. Now I need to add that this is just one area where my husband struggles; he excels in most other areas. He is a supportive husband, a loving father and a faithful partner to walk through life with.

I'd love to tell you that that was the last time we faced this conflict but that would be a lie. As I write this, my husband is between jobs again. We are eight years into 'the plan' and he has had over 20 jobs – 20 jobs! Do you ever get the feeling God is trying to teach you something . . . and you are missing the lesson?

The first big jump lasted months, during which I was terrified we would lose our home. There was a fear inside of homelessness and raising our kids in poverty. But God provided. We never missed a payment. How?

God taught me that I could trust him to provide for us, even when I couldn't see how. He also taught me how to forgive my past and surrender our finances to him.

A changing response

The next time, I responded differently. I had grown so much in my relationship with God and he was teaching me to pray more than I complained. Bud walked in, ready for a fight: he found grace instead. It went this way:

'Tiffany, I quit my job today,' he mumbled.

'Do you have another job to go to tomorrow like you promised?' I replied, with my face hidden while I tried to hide the tears.

'No. I'm sorry,' he nearly cried in reply.

'I trust that you wouldn't do anything intentionally to hurt our family. God will take care of us,' I honestly encouraged.

'Are we OK?' he asked as he hesitantly walked towards me at the kitchen sink.

'You are my husband. My love for you is not based on how well you provide financially for our family. I love that you are funny and honest and caring. This won't help us get ahead, but as long as we are together, we are OK.' I hugged him and we both cried for a while.

Through the next several months, as Bud looked for work, God taught me that I could bring my every need to him. I could hope in him and believe in him, even when I was struggling to love my husband well.

God has given me a lot of opportunities to practise how to react in love rather than respond from fear to my husband's choices.

Extending grace to our partner's mistakes

Conflict often stems from one or both of us making an unwise choice, causing the other spouse to react emotionally.

What if you take the emotion out of the way you react to unwise choices?

Two humans living life together are prone to make unwise choices from time to time. When I mess up, I need grace and understanding. My husband is no different. God has been teaching me that even our biggest mistakes, when met with grace, can be overcome.

A godly wife extends grace instead of emotional abuse . . . just like Jesus.

At every twist in our story, when I want to be angry with my husband for his mistakes, God points me back to the cross. God reminds me to trust him, do marriage his way, extend grace and love and honour even when they are not deserved. Why? Because that's how he loves me.

Yes, conflict happens in marriage. There are things that catch us off guard and rock our world. At the heart of conflict is at least one child of God who has messed up and needs the grace to get back up off the ground and try again. As Bud's wife, it is my joy and privilege to extend that grace, to remind him he is not the sum of his mistakes and he can and will do better next time.

Extending grace when conflict arises is not easy. When my husband messes up, it affects us all. Giving those feelings to God and trusting that he has us, regardless of how badly my husband messes up, is a spiritual discipline learned over time. Even when my husband is far from God, when I am drawing near, he promises to catch us. As a bonus, every time I extend grace, I see my husband draw near to God as well (because I make sure to give God credit for that grace).

This is the life we live – two imperfect people who made vows to love until death do us part. Conflict does not nullify those vows. The love and grace of God give us the strength to love through conflict and come out the other side more holy and satisfied in him.

A few years ago, God called Tiffany to become the mentor that she needed in the beginning, and she now coaches wives online at http://www.hopejoyinchrist.com. Through her blog and utilizing books and Bible study resources, she teaches what it means to be a godly wife and how the principles of Scripture can rescue marriages today.

Over to you

- Think about how you each handle conflict. Could there be inner beliefs fuelling your responses? Discuss and pray about these if so.
- Is one of you more confrontational than the other? Think about how you can extend grace to one another in times of conflict.
- Have you ever considered your heart attitude during times of conflict? What action might you need to do in response to what God has pinpointed in your heart as you've read this chapter?

Grace Takes Responsibility

Do not be deceived: God cannot be mocked. A man reaps what he sows. Whoever sows to please their flesh, from the flesh will reap destruction; whoever sows to please the Spirit, from the Spirit will reap eternal life.

Galatians 6:7–8

Claire: As I said earlier, while it took a lot of pain for me to discover it, I realized that I abdicated a lot of responsibility in my life. I had looked to Steve to a certain extent for my spiritual wellbeing. I also looked to him to fulfil my overall, basic sense of contentment. How wrong I was! We don't get married in order to be fulfilled (it's far too hard a journey!), in order to be 'completed' or to become content. Those things are only ever found in God, and whatever we put in his place – be it our partner, career, kids or anything else – is an idol that blocks our intimacy with him. And I think that is, ultimately, why I lived on a self-destruct course for so long – because I had never recognized my heart's idolatry for what it was. I was too caught up in being the victim, and looking for the comfort and approval of others, to see how far I had veered in that direction.

As I was writing a Bible study guide on Exodus recently, I was struck afresh at how clear God is about idols and worshipping him alone:

> You shall have no other gods before me. You shall not make for yourself an image in the form of anything in heaven above or on the earth beneath or in the waters below. You shall not bow down to them or worship them; for I, the LORD your God, am a jealous God, punishing the children for the sin of the parents to the third and fourth generation of those who hate me, but showing love to a thousand generations of those who love me and keep my commandments.
>
> Exodus 20:3–4

God takes idolatry incredibly seriously, and yet I know I have entertained all sorts of idols in my life without really thinking about them. Things like my job, my relationship with Steve, my kids, my roles in church – even time-fillers such as reading, TV and Facebook. It is quite easy to fall into idolatrous ways, which is probably why God spoke against idolatry so vehemently. He wants us to take this issue seriously. It is vital that we each make time to come before God in an attitude of humility to ask him, as David did: 'Search me, God, and know my heart; test me and know my anxious thoughts. See if there is any offensive way in me, and lead me in the way everlasting' (Ps. 139:23–24).

Marriage as a means of sanctification

In all honesty, it is only fairly recently (more than 25 years into marriage!) that I've really understood how marriage is such

> When life is going well, we can stop bothering to make an effort; when it is extra hard, we may feel we have no energy left for anything else.

an important part of our sanctification. Living with someone so closely, sharing intimately – physically but also mentally, emotionally and spiritually – exposes our shortcomings. The really ugly parts of us come out in daily life; either as we face the monotony of the mundane or the surprising pain of unexpected turmoil. When life is going well, we can stop bothering to make an effort; when it is extra hard, we may feel we have no energy left for anything else.[1]

It isn't just our shortcomings that are exposed – so too are those of our partner. We may find ourselves being shocked by some of their behaviour, as well as our own. We may also find it hard to love them on their less than lovely days. But what was Jesus' teaching on loving one another? He went far beyond just loving God – he taught that we should love our neighbour as much as ourselves (Matt. 22:34–40). Who lives more closely to us than our spouse? Jesus actually went even further than that. He also taught us to love our enemies (Matt. 5:43–48). We may not immediately think of our spouses when we read those verses, but the truth is we need to learn to keep on loving despite their, and our, ugliness. Even through arguments, differences of opinions, when we feel we've been the only one doing all the sacrificing lately . . .

It has taken me a long time, but I have finally understood a bit of advice that my mum gave me much earlier in our marriage: 'When you are desperately looking for your husband to change, you are looking at the wrong person.' My mum was married to my dad for many, many years after becoming a Christian. She cried out to God to change behaviour in my dad many times – and yet she always felt God gently nudge her to look at herself instead.

This little nugget of wisdom has caused me no end of strife, but that's mainly because it has forced me to look at the less than pretty aspects of my character. We know it is said that opposites attract and, even though we have so many similarities because we spent our teenage years growing up together, Steve and I are definitely opposites in a great many areas. That means we do complement each other, and work really well as a team as we each strengthen the other's weaker points. However, in all honesty, his opposite approach to so many things can really niggle me regularly (including the way we've written this book – I'm so much more methodical; he much more relaxed!). I can complain about the things that really grate on me, and plead with God to change him. And yet, deep down in my heart, I know that it is my attitude that needs to change. Often Steve is not 'sinning' – he just approaches life in a very different way to me.

I know that I can have a tendency to moan, and to point out the things I find difficult about Steve. And yet the Bible says to 'take captive every thought to make it obedient to Christ' (2 Cor. 10:5). This is a verse that I often use during speaking engagements, as I am certain that we don't stop and think very often about what we are feeding our minds. But if I remembered to apply this to each grumble and complaint there would be a very different result!

Praying to be soft towards your partner is a dangerous prayer to pray, as it often entails a painful process for yourself, but it is essential. Humility and malleability are such necessary qualities within marriage. As is learning to take responsibility for our mistakes and say sorry quickly.

The latter is something I can find quite difficult, as this story will reveal. On our wedding day, our youth pastor (who was giving the address) showed he understood my character well when he turned to Steve and said: 'In an argument you will have to say sorry first – because Claire never will.' Everyone laughed, I was slightly embarrassed – but what is even more embarrassing is the fact that I clung on to that statement and threw it back at Steve whenever we were arguing in the early years of our marriage. I used it as an excuse not to own up when it was time for me to say sorry.

Becoming more self-aware

While it is true that we are no longer under law, but grace, God does expect us to work out our 'salvation with fear and trembling' (Phil. 2:12). Paul spoke of the need for extreme self-discipline in 1 Corinthians 9 when he said: 'I do not run like someone running aimlessly; I do not fight like a boxer beating the air. No, I strike a blow to my body and make it my slave so that after I have preached to others, I myself will not be disqualified for the prize' (vv.26–27).

To me, this talks of the necessity of self-awareness. What is it that we know can cause us to stumble – that can make us less than loving towards our partner? Once we are aware of those things, what do we do to stop ourselves from falling? Jesus knew how easily sin entangles, and how it is progressive too. We might think something is pretty harmless but, if we allow ourselves to linger too long on an unhelpful TV programme or website page, we soon become immune to its effects on us.

Just consider how David, the man God described as being after his own heart, spent too long lingering in the place where he had a full view of temptation. He didn't simply wake up one day and choose to take Bathsheba for himself, cause her to commit adultery too and then cover things up by ensuring her husband was killed on the battlefield. There was a progression to his sin.

Jesus had some pretty radical suggestions for how to deal with such sin, such as:

> You have heard that it was said, 'You shall not commit adultery.' But I tell you that anyone who looks at a woman lustfully has already committed adultery with her in his heart. If your right eye causes you to stumble, gouge it out and throw it away. It is better for you to lose one part of your body than for your whole body to be thrown into hell.
>
> Matthew 5:27–29

Ouch! We don't like things that make us uncomfortable, do we? But we don't like it when our partner's ongoing unhealthy habits and/or sins impact us, so we need to ensure that we are working on our own. But how do we become more aware of them? After all, it is often much easier to spot the flaws in those around us than in ourselves, isn't it?

I think that is why we can often live with character flaws in ourselves without even recognizing they are there. We can do the same with the effects of emotional pain from the past too, and yet, if we don't deal with the hurt, and simply bury it, those emotions have nowhere to go. At some point, they will make their way out again, either through a possibly unconnected emotional outburst, when our partner, or someone else, gets more than they bargained for, or through mental or physical ill health. We damage ourselves, and those around us, when we either view difficulties as weak and therefore needing to be squashed, or too painful and embarrassing to admit to. We have a responsibility to work through past pain whenever God makes us aware of it, so that the past will no longer be able to affect us, and our marriage (see Malcolm and Kim's story in Chapter 3).

Steve: As Claire mentioned, we need to take responsibility for what we allow ourselves to look at. So many Christian marriages are being undermined by broken trust, guilt and shame that immediately brings distance between partners, but also with God. The sheer accessibility of porn, coupled with the privacy in which we can now access it, provides a toxic cocktail that destroys intimacy and, sadly, often marriages. What begins as curiosity ends up enslaving. Whatever your track record with porn has been, know that you are not alone in your struggle with it – but also that you simply cannot be complacent about it.

The story of David and Bathsheba teaches us how to guard our own hearts. Firstly, we need to acknowledge that none of us is immune. King David, a mighty warrior king who wrote nearly half the Psalms, gave in to lustful desires. Secondly, we are vulnerable when we are bored. David should have been leading his people in battle, yet he abdicated that responsibility to Joab. When we abdicate our responsibility to lead ourselves, we take our eye off the ball and become vulnerable to temptation. As Christians, all of us are in a spiritual battle and we need to recognize when and where we are vulnerable. If you knew your house was about to be burgled you would immediately check the vulnerable access points. You would strengthen that vulnerable ground floor window. You'd make access difficult to that low flat roof. You

> When we abdicate our responsibility to lead ourselves, we take our eye off the ball and become vulnerable to temptation.

would also keep watch vigilantly. In the same way, we need to ask ourselves: where and when am I vulnerable to porn and what are my triggers? Is it when I'm bored, as David probably was, or tired after a long day? It is when I am in a bad place emotionally? Or is it when I look at certain social media sites? I don't believe any Christian husband or wife starts out with the decision to break trust and covenant with their partner and become trapped in the cycle of thrill, shame, repentance . . . and repeat. Yet that is sadly the experience of so many. We each need to take responsibility. We have placed filters over our internet connection so that any device in our house is covered, in order to protect ourselves and our children from accessing any unhelpful sites.

Accountability is also key. It is often said that sin grows in the dark. Add an unhealthy dose of shame into the mix and you end up with men and women enslaved to habits for years. As their pastor, people have asked me to be accountable for their internet browsing history. There are several apps now that email a web browsing report to a trusted friend. This is such a wise thing to do. But we also need to open up the conversation about this issue – again with trusted friends – and not allow shame to keep it hidden and left to fester. One of the joys of being a pastor is seeing people finally released from years of shame as they have opened up, confessed and received the beautiful gift of God's forgiveness.

Practical ways to be responsible for ourselves daily

Claire: In recent years, I have found spiritual practices such as the Daily Examen an incredibly helpful way of keeping myself accountable before God each day. As an evangelical Christian,

I didn't grow up learning any spiritual practices – in fact, when my mum accepted Jesus she left the Anglican Church soon after and so I viewed anything traditional as weighed down by law, rather than grace. However, I've come to learn that utilizing such practices draws me closer to Jesus and positions my heart into an attitude of humility and teachability.

It was Sharon Brown's fictional series Sensible Shoes[2] that opened my eyes to spiritual disciplines – and for that, I am exceedingly grateful to her. In the first book, of the same name as the series, she describes the Examen simply as an opportunity to sit with Jesus and look back over our day. Developed by Ignatius of Loyola back in the 16th century, the Examen is a discipline many Christians use twice daily – at noon and in the evening. I have tended to only do it once a day, but I can see the wisdom in taking time in the middle of the day – as it could change attitudes and, indeed, the overall direction of the rest of the day.

The premise of the Examen is to slow down, prepare our hearts and invite the Holy Spirit to guide us as we look back, noticing the little details that we might otherwise miss but which can teach us so much. (Sharon refers to it as viewing our lives like a movie on playback.) With an attitude of thankfulness for what God has blessed us with, we can also notice when our emotions were perhaps stirred more negatively. Were there times when we were really aware of God's presence – and other times when he didn't seem close by?

We can take the moments when perhaps we were provoked to anger and hurt by someone and bring whatever confessions of repentance are needed before God, as well as sitting still to receive his healing and forgiveness. Before finishing, we can focus on one particular aspect of our day and bring it before

God in prayer, as well as looking forward and asking for his help to be attentive to his presence the next day.

Having practised this (on and off), I was able to recognize when I had a pretty strong reaction to what other people were saying to me recently. Rather than simply getting upset, I also took it before God prayerfully and asked him to show me what was behind my response. Chatting it through with Steve, we both had a similar revelation about it at the same time. That is not something I would have done in the past (I've always been a 'let's not go digging for things' kind of person). However, I've really sensed the Holy Spirit guiding me to slow down and reminding me to use such spiritual practices when they will be particularly useful. Perhaps the Examen may be a way you can take more responsibility for your own spiritual walk . . .[3]

There is nothing quite like Scripture for piercing our souls – after all it is: 'alive and active. Sharper than any double-edged sword, it penetrates even to dividing soul and spirit, joints and marrow; it judges the thoughts and attitudes of the heart' (Heb. 4:12). Making time to delve into it for ourselves daily is so important. I try to do a mixture of shorter readings with Bible study notes and longer studies, where I try and work hard myself at deciphering the meaning and allowing it to speak into my life directly. It helps that I regularly write Bible study notes, as I find God speaks to me hugely as I'm preparing them!

I also find books by trusted writers immensely helpful when learning more about God and myself. When God has provided revelation to someone and they write it down in a way that makes it tangible and relevant to our lives it is a real gift. I sometimes have those jaw-dropping moments, either when someone seems to just 'get' exactly where I'm at, or when their words get right to the heart of something God is putting his finger on in my life.

I had one of those latter moments recently. I was reading *Invitation to the Jesus Life*[4] by Jan Johnson and was on the chapter about speaking the truth in love. Having already confessed that I find positive affirmation quite difficult to speak out, you will probably have already guessed that there was much I was finding challenging in the chapter. Then I arrived at the questions for discussion and reflection. I only got as far as the first question, in which she asked: 'In what ways does contempt leak from you?' What followed was a table with various behaviours listed, such as sarcasm, playing the victim, passive-aggressive behaviour, grumbling, withdrawing – I took a sharp intake of breath when I realized that, even though I have spent time specifically trying to work on this area, I could recognize most of the list in myself. I found that a little depressing, to be honest, but decided, rather than allowing myself to spiral, to take it to God and ask for his help to view myself as he does. I realized afresh that negativity is still my natural tendency and that, while Steve is there to support, encourage and, yes, gently correct when necessary, it is down to me to keep working on this, with Jesus.

I have also found the passage in Colossians 3 about dressing ourselves with the right qualities incredibly challenging over the years (I was first writing blogs about it in 2012!). At certain times, I've used the verses as a prayer in the mornings, focusing on consciously 'putting on' kindness, compassion, humility, etc. at the same time as I dress my body with clothes. Here's what it says in verses 12–13 (in *The Message* translation, because I find the wording particularly striking):

> So, chosen by God for this new life of love, dress in the wardrobe God picked out for you: compassion, kindness, humility, quiet strength, discipline. Be even-tempered, content with

second place, quick to forgive an offense. Forgive as quickly and completely as the Master forgave you. And regardless of what else you put on, wear love. It's your basic, all-purpose garment. Never be without it.

Just take a moment to imagine what your marriage (and other relationships) could look like if you took the time to 'dress' your spirit with these attitudes. Looking through the verses again, there is so much rich wisdom contained within them. Our marriages desperately need us to be humble, kind, compassionate, etc. But also 'content with second place'. As we will come to look at later (in Chapter 10), there will be times when we need to be happy to take a step back in order for our partner to move forward into the spotlight. Are you content to value your partner above yourself, looking to their interests above your own (as Phil. 2:3 teaches us to)? And are you quick to forgive? I have learned how much it unlocks grace, not only in our marriage, but in my own life and beyond too.

Pursuing God for myself

Liz Holden and her husband Dave, who heads up New Ground (part of the Newfrontiers family of churches), have supported us in our ministries over the years. After Steve heard Liz speak at a church-planting conference about learning to take responsibility for her walk with God during the early part of their marriage, we asked whether she would share her story here.

I have to say that getting married was not in my original plan when I renewed my relationship with Jesus, after seven years of being away from God. I was so thrilled to be back in the love of my heavenly Father, and had so much to learn, that the last thing I needed was to get emotionally involved with someone. I became a member of my local church and had some fantastic mature Christians who were discipling me and getting me back on track in my Christian life. Many new and wonderful discoveries awaited me, mainly being personally filled with the Holy Spirit, understanding the doctrine of the grace of God, and having a fresh passion for the local church.

I became a nurse in the community and had my new life sorted, but God had another plan. I met David, we fell in love, got engaged after six weeks and married within six months. This entailed me moving to south-east London to join David, who had been leading a new church for about a year. Suddenly I was in a new environment, a new church and married to the church pastor. The church was growing and many younger than us were becoming Christians and needing care and discipleship.

These were exciting days, but also challenging, as I was still developing my own personal walk with God. I started to feel a certain level of insecurity that I wasn't meeting people's expectations of me and that my husband was way ahead of me in spiritual matters. This showed up when we prayed together, and I would feel a sense of inadequacy and even embarrassment at my lack of eloquence!

I remember telling David how I felt, and he suggested we stopped praying together until I felt comfortable to do it and that I should simply get on and enjoy my walk with God. That was what I needed to hear; no pressure to pretend but the encouragement to pursue my knowledge of God for myself. Being open and honest with each other was the best thing because, although a bit painful, it helped us to be more understanding and patient.

Nothing to prove; everything to enjoy

I started to experience the grace of God in my life. I realized that God had called me, a prodigal daughter, back at this very specific time in my life. It had been his initiative, not mine, and he knew the future path ahead of me, so I could trust him with it.

My identity as a Christian was something I needed to apply to myself – no one else could do that for me – and how much more helpful to David I would be as I grew in confidence in my identity in Christ. Reading the Bible became essential daily bread for me and I would steal Bible commentaries from David's study.

Of course we soon got back to praying together, as I was the only one putting pressure on myself. I realized that through the grace of God I had nothing to prove, and everything to enjoy!

Learning total dependency

In the following few years, as the church grew, there were many joys and also many pressures and challenges. A few months after we married my mother died, which I found devastating; she had prayed me back to God and had been the most loving, stable force in my life. As I prayed about it, I was made aware that God had provided for me in David, a life companion and soul mate at a time when I wasn't ready for one . . . or so I thought.

We also faced stressful times in church life and illness, as David was ill for a year, and we had our first child. Suddenly I was the strong one and carrying the responsibility for the home and our daily life. It was during this season that I would say that my faith really grew. Total dependency on God comes when you don't have any of your own resources left, and you don't have the time or energy to feel inadequate.

Asking the Holy Spirit to give me strength in the heat of the battle and trusting in the promises of God by applying them to my circumstances was like putting one foot in front of the other, by faith.

God's all-sufficient grace

God has provided me with his grace through each season of my married life, as he promises in 2 Corinthians 12:9: 'My grace is sufficient for you, for my power is made perfect in weakness.' We have both needed to rely on that grace individually and take responsibility for our own personal walk with God. Together we have proved God's grace towards us time and time again, as we have humbled ourselves under his generous hand, and allowed him to show us where we need to change, where we need to forgive and where we need to endure. And, because it's all his grace, which is freely given, where we need to laugh!

Know what pushes your buttons

Claire: I know that I find everything – including our relationship and family life – more difficult when I am tired. I need to have a good eight hours sleep a night to function well and be at my best emotionally. However, I spent a long time believing and therefore living out the idea that as a church-leading couple we needed to be busy. I felt we couldn't ask others to work hard all day and then come out to events or lead areas of ministry if we weren't doing the same. In the early years of our church, out of necessity we were either attending meetings or preparing for them in some way every evening of each week. There were times when I felt spiritually dry, but I rode those out generally. I loved the fact that Steve and I were working so much more closely – but there were moments when I felt there was no space and time for us as a couple; it was always work, work, work. Those feelings of loneliness and resentment would rise up and I would struggle to serve out of the right attitude.

And then I hit my forties. I hadn't noticed, but gradually my body had been trying to tell me that I couldn't keep up the same pace I had in my thirties. And actually God didn't want me to. There were others he had raised up to do some of the things I was doing, and I needed to give them room. I was becoming tired (and snappier) more quickly, and as our children got a bit older, I found the issues they needed me to address were more complex too. So my evenings were more difficult to manage and I was going to bed too late, absolutely exhausted.

I listened a little . . . but not enough. And so God *made* me listen. A couple of years ago I started having problems with the hearing in one ear. I noticed my foldback sounded muffled when I played keyboard and sang on a Sunday morning. When I got my ear checked out, I was told that my hearing was still in the 'normal' range but they had also discovered a perforation that they advised me to get fixed. So I started the next New Year in hospital having an operation. And I discovered I have the same vile response to anaesthetic that my mum did. It was a short operation and supposedly a quick recovery, but I was incredibly nauseous for a while afterwards and also needed to rest – a lot. When I went back after six months to be signed off, they tested my hearing again – but it was the same as it had been before the operation (which they had warned me was a possibility).

I went home rather dejected. I'd had a lot of prayer for healing before the operation, so my question for God was: 'Why did I have to have the operation?' And I heard him say very clearly in my mind: 'It was all about getting you to slow down.' I wished I'd listened and responded more fully beforehand once I heard that! But it did cause me to have an honest conversation with Steve about the fact that I could no longer continue to live at the pace that we had been; I felt we needed to pare back what we were doing in the evenings – and we have drastically changed the amount we take on now.

Steve and I are opposites in this whole area: it may be partly because his body was conditioned throughout his twenties to work through the night, but he wakes up when the clock strikes 10 – and he can easily work away beyond midnight. I, on the other hand, struggle to stay awake past 10.30, although, if I do push through the barrier, I can then keep going but I suffer immensely the next day, as do those around me! I have had to learn, on those nights when he really isn't ready to come to bed at the same time, that I have to put my health and wellbeing first and go to bed at a reasonable time (see below for more on this).

Allowing one another – and others – to speak into our lives

While I believe we each need to take responsibility for our own walks before God, he has gifted us with a spouse, and that is one of the main ways that he rubs the sharp edges off of us! Simply by living with someone that is so different from us causes friction at times, which, if we submit ourselves to his loving hand, can be used by God to shape us. And in a relation-ship that is hopefully full of trust, encouragement and mutual championing we can also learn to gently correct one another when we feel God prompts us to.

I have a natural tendency to try and change those living with me. I can tell myself that I'm teaching my children to take responsibility for themselves (I am to a certain extent), and my husband to show the same consideration I'm asking them all to, but there are times my 'correction' simply comes out of the annoyance of having to pick up after them for the millionth time. So I know I don't need to be reminded to bring correction – I need to stop and think whose correction it is I'm trying to bring when I feel the need to!

Having said that, I do try and be aware of when God is prompting me to highlight something, as I know this is an important part of us supporting one another in our marriage (see Chapter 7). More often than not God asks me to correct Steve's image of himself after a church service, when he might feel things haven't gone as he wanted them to. So the correction involves bringing encouragement to help him realign his thinking with God's. Sometimes it involves gently inviting him to see things a different way; I have more of a compassionate heart that can become aware of when others are suffering – Steve is more of a creative visionary who may not pick up on all those details.

I don't find being corrected by Steve easy at all though. I know it is the sin in me that pushes back, not wanting him to be the agent of God's discipline. But the way that correction is done has a big impact too; loving gentleness rather than gruff condescension is so important. When we can see that the other person has our best interests at heart, rather than their own agenda, it makes it much easier to listen to and reflect upon what they are saying.

God has also surrounded us with family and friends for mutual care. Cultivating close friendships with people should provide us with an opportunity both to support and challenge them, but also to receive the same from them. I know that I personally really value the friendships I have that allow me to open up and confess when I'm struggling – and often even the act of describing my thoughts (sometimes my thoughts towards Steve) helps me to take responsibility and do something about them. I also know those people are championing me and will keep what I've told them in confidence before God in prayer.

Taking responsibility for the marriage together

As we have said, we have an enemy who detests marriage, and will try all sorts of strategies to disarm and destroy yours. Do you know where your weak points are? Have you ever discussed them? Over the years we have had to have long, hard discussions about how Claire can tend to feel lonely or uncherished, and what we've both needed to do to ensure that doesn't happen – and, when it does, that we don't fall into sin (such as Claire looking to another person to make herself feel like she is wanted or needed). We've also talked about Steve's laid-back attitude to working hours; that he is quite happy to continue working long into the night, even when it fuels Claire's feeling of being alone. While Steve is a night bird, and often does some of his best work late at night, when he hears Claire mentioning that she is finding that tough, he makes an effort to go to bed at the same time as her.

You will have your own thoughts on what is best to protect your marriage. Having lived through a near break-up that happened when a friendship that started innocently enough took over Claire's life, we are now very guarded about relationships with the opposite sex.

It may be that one of you has struggled with a particular issue – say pornography or, as we read about below, an eating disorder. There may be practical steps that you need to agree together in order to safeguard both yourself and your relationship.

Facing the ugliness with courage

Emma Scrivener has battled anorexia and depression twice – once as a teenager, but then again after marrying Glen. As a marriage partner of someone going through such an ordeal, how do you deal with the ugly truth each and every day, ground down and feeling powerless and alone each time your partner makes a poor choice? Both Emma and Glen share very honestly about the effect that anorexia has had on their marriage.

Emma: We were both finishing Bible college, and I began to feel completely overwhelmed by the prospect of a new church and what would be a new role as a pastor's wife. I simply couldn't cope, and my response was to stop eating.

Anorexia is *not* glamorous. It's hair falling out; nails turning black; internal organs shutting down; fine, silver hair growing all over your face and body; chest pains; shivering cold all the time; constant hunger, exhaustion and hyperactivity. It's collapsing on the way to the bathroom and soiling yourself, unable to get up.[5]

By the end I could barely walk. Nobody seemed to be able to reach me, and nothing anyone did helped.

Learning the hard lessons
Glen: I learned the hard way that it is vital for the other partner in the marriage to understand that their partner is bound; yes, initially they did make those bad choices, but they get to a point of being trapped and can't simply change because we ask them

to. They aren't doing any of their self-destructive behaviours on purpose to spite us. It is vital we understand this – and also vital that we continue to wrestle in prayer for them. I know that when I didn't pray, Emma suffered.

I learned, too, that I needed to change some of my own behaviour and take responsibility, as I recognized that I actually enabled Emma's downward spiral. When we got married, I basically thought that love meant saying 'Yes' to my wife, no matter what. If she wanted poison . . . well, what's a loving husband to do but give her poison? That's a stupid analogy but only because it highlights the stupidity of what I was doing. I took no lead in casting a vision for what healthy desires and directions might look like in our marriage. In the absence of this Emma demanded more and more of her own way, and I conceded more and more to drives that were ultimately self-destructive. I had – and at times still have – immense difficulty saying 'No', especially to desires that come from the desperation of addiction. Part of recovery meant *me* discovering a voice in the marriage and convictions on where we needed to go.[6]

The need for community

Glen and Emma: We both adamantly believe that when couples are going through such intense struggles they need community, even when that can be a hard call. While you may be sorely tempted to cut yourselves off, particularly if you are faced with friends in church who don't understand what you are going through, you simply cannot manage this on your own. Unhealthy patterns will become normal to you when you try to manage by yourselves.

Glen: I recognize now that far too often I coddled Emma in the darkness when I should have been moving her into the light of community. It is immensely difficult to make a judgement call on that; I found that to particularly be the case when she had become afraid of others and wanted to know that I was safe. But it is vital to be committed to life in community and you need to do all you can to move you both towards that.

For any other spouse facing such difficulties with their partner I would say, make sure that you receive from Jesus each and every day. And allow him to work on your own sins. Get, or stay, in community. Love your partner – and pray without ceasing. Jesus is the one that can redeem the situation – you can't, but you *are* called to engage in the daily mess.

If you want to read more about their story, Emma has written very honestly about her own struggles in her book A New Name, *and both have shared openly on her website: https://emmascrivener.net.*

The power of prayer

One of the most powerful things you can do to protect your marriage is also one of the things we have struggled with the most: pray for your marriage (both separately and together). Each time we do marriage preparation classes with an engaged couple we are reminded of how important this is and, while we have made progress, we recognize we need to take more responsibility for this area yet again.

As we began our married life leading separate lives, we never got into the habit of praying together regularly. And so, while we make the effort to do so now, it can at times still seem somewhat alien and awkward. While we may be really comfortable praying with others at church, or with and for our friends, praying as a couple has never been easy.

When we take the time to pray for our marriages we are declaring God's rule and reign over them and his sovereignty. We are acknowledging our need for his help, but also declaring our trust in him. Praying also gives God the space to offer his wisdom and counsel to us, as well as his encouragement. We don't navigate marriage alone – as the marriage ceremony often cites: 'A cord of three strands is not quickly broken' (Eccl. 4:12) so it makes sense to invite him as often as possible to offer us advice.

When we are praying regularly, it is harder to hold grudges, and easier to sacrificially love the other person. How often do you pray for your partner's walk with God? For their development as a person? For their relationship with you, and also with those close to you? For their job and/or calling? For protection over them as they go about their day? The latter is something our children have grown up hearing, as we made it a part of our daily prayer in the car on the way to school, praying God's peace and protection over each one of us and our days. Prayer is such a powerful weapon; we need to learn to use it to fight for our marriages daily.

Over to you

- Are there areas of your own life that you know you have allowed yourself to get slack over? Take some time before God to repent and seek his guidance.
- Are there areas in your marriage where one or other of you is avoiding taking responsibility? Bring those before God now.
- Thinking back to what was said about clothing our spirits with the right attitudes, here is a poem Claire wrote based on Colossians 3 when her biological dad got married again a few years ago, which she read out during the ceremony. Take some time to read and reflect on it, thinking about whether your default is to find fault or

to love your partner each day. Then discuss how you can encourage one another to put on these qualities, and reflect love to one another, with your partner:

I stand at the wardrobe, choosing my outfit carefully;
Ensuring it matches to create the look I'm after today.
But do I choose my attitudes so carefully?
Do I ever consider how I clothe myself with them?

When I look over to say good morning to you,
Is it love that is covering my words?
Or is there a hint of tension or anger within them,
Left over from a difficult conversation yesterday?

How do I react to you throughout the day –
When I'm busy, harassed, trying to get things done?
Is love still clothing my attitudes, my words, my actions?
If they were cut open would love be running through?

What about compassion, patience and gentleness?
Do I forgive quickly if you offend me?
Am I careful not to point out your shortcomings;
Those moments when you do things differently to me?

I choose today to not only clothe my body, but to consider
    my attitudes too.
I choose today to put on love above all else,
To actively cultivate the best of attitudes towards you.
Will you choose to love me in this way too?

Grace is Dying to Self

For whoever wants to save their life will lose it, but whoever loses their life for me will find it.

Matthew 16:25

Marriage is a way that God refines us, sanctifies us and teaches us that the world does not revolve around us (which is what our western culture seeks to make us believe every day). Marriage helps us on a daily basis to realize we are here for others.

As we saw in the last chapter, in an honest marriage relationship your faults are exposed and pointed out. We each need to learn to be honest about those, accept the need to change and to submit to God over and over again.

Recognizing the lie

Claire: One of the biggest cultural lies that we need to address is that marriage is there for our fulfilment. I know that I bought into that myth and was full of romantic ideals when I entered marriage. That is probably why I crashed so hard when I realized what the reality is truly like. It didn't match up to my (selfish) expectations – at all.

Today our culture teaches us that the world should be all about *our* individual truth, *our* individual needs and wants. With such an 'I-centred' approach to life in general, this will inevitably rub off onto the way that we approach marriage. When we were about five years into our marriage, we saw how this attitude really permeates our culture. I went to the doctor because at the time I was suffering from what was diagnosed as chronic fatigue syndrome. I was finding Steve's hours personally gruelling. He was working around the clock, often only coming home as I was setting out to catch a train the next morning. Each night I lay awake hour after hour, desperately trying to welcome sleep, then waking after a few short hours of rest to start my working day. When I tried to talk to my doctor about this, to see if she had any practical ideas about what could help me, she replied (without any hint of sarcasm or humour): 'Well I think it is about time you got yourself a new husband!' I was totally shocked, and started seeing a different doctor.

Looking back now, I can see I allowed myself to listen to the same message over and over; it was simply dressed up differently. I spent much more time with work colleagues than church friends during that period of our lives and the main message I got from them was that I should let my hair down and simply do what I wanted to do; I couldn't be blamed because my husband had basically abandoned me. I lapped that up because it fed my selfish desires, and gave me an excuse for either feeding the bitterness or acting inappropriately.

Only sticking around for a marriage while it is benefiting us personally is far from a biblical approach. But it is important to recognize that generations are now growing up hearing this message daily. And new Christians may not understand where it falls short of a biblical view. That is why we need to model marriages in which both partners die to self . . . daily. And we should not be afraid to preach about the need for sacrifice in all relationships, including marriage.

Jesus taught: 'Whoever wants to be my disciple must deny themselves and take up their cross and follow me' (Matt. 16:24) and Romans 6:6 says: 'For we know that our old self was crucified with him so that the body ruled by sin might be done away with, that we should no longer be slaves to sin'.

We believe that marriage is one of the means by which we learn to die to ourselves. And, if we approach our marriage with a self-sacrificing attitude, it allows both of us to really blossom. Without the selfish attitude of 'what can this relationship do for me?' we each learn the joy of giving of ourselves to the other – and what it means to receive that same gift back from our partner. We actually have the daily opportunity to put someone else above ourselves through the way we interact with our spouse.

In Chapter 5 we looked at how we need to take the time to understand one another, as we will have different approaches and outlooks. Sometimes (often in fact), our dying to self will necessitate putting the other person's needs (and even wants) above our own. This is something I would say Steve is pretty good at. He knows that I find driving difficult, and that I'm a bit of a technophobe. Even though it puts him out, he will gladly drive me whenever he can. And he is the exact opposite to me when it comes to technology, so I have my very own in-house IT consultant for those times when my computer or phone does something unexpected.

But there are times when dying to ourselves is incredibly painful; when it seems like the last thing we want to do. If we are both going through difficult seasons we can get tired, irritable and simply want to take a break from it all – and yet sticking by, and sacrificing for, each other in those moments means that they can end up being the times of biggest transformation. We have taken great encouragement from and been challenged by Jeff and Sarah Walton's writing, as they have learned this through the most intense suffering, and so we asked them to share some of their thoughts on dying to self here.

> Sticking by, and sacrificing for, each other in those moments means that they can end up being the times of biggest transformation.

Dying to self in the midst of chronic illness

Jeff and Sarah Walton have had to face chronic illness not just in one but in five members of their family. Based in America, this has had huge implications for them financially, as they have navigated paying for necessary medication and treatments. Here they describe honestly the effect that has had on their marriage, and how they have had to learn to die to self.

Jeff: Our first child arrived less than three years after we were married. At seven weeks old, he developed a fever and ended up with life-altering neurological challenges that caused his behaviour to change in a bewildering way. Sarah's health began declining too; with each of the four children she bore, her own chronic pain and illness increased, and an old ankle injury from high school has also meant the need for five surgeries.

Eventually, each of our children began to exhibit symptoms of chronic illness and doctors worked out that each of them has Lyme disease, as does Sarah. As things got progressively worse, and our marriage was beginning to suffer, it was obvious that I could no longer sustain my job as a consultant to orthopaedic surgeons. So I left it, which meant we lost half our income. We had to sell our dream home and rent a smaller one. Then the new company I had joined began to struggle, and I was left without a job at all.

At this point, we realized we were in crisis. As a couple, all we ever did was navigate doctors, difficult behaviour and trying to soothe hurting children, alongside my wife's chronic pain. We were broken and wondering why God was letting us face all of this.

While we had known our marriage wouldn't be perfect, we just weren't prepared for how much suffering would hit our lives and marriage. At first, we just put our heads down and kept going, but as time went on and we both grew weary, tension and distance began to grow because neither of us had the energy to do anything but survive.

Physical and emotional struggles

Sarah: The most difficult symptom I deal with day to day is body aches, similar to when you have the flu. Needless to say, it's not only difficult to care for the kids and our home, and be present in my marriage, it's incredibly difficult to do so with patience and joy. But what this has done more than anything is drive me to Christ, pleading for his strength to endure and carry the load he has given me. Not only that, but it has driven me to the gospel over and over when I fail, understanding what Christ did for me on the cross in a more profound way. And, by his grace, he is gradually strengthening my faith muscles and giving me greater endurance on those days that I battle pain, enabling me to love and serve my family in his strength and rest in his grace when I just can't physically do what I wish I could be doing.

There are times when I reach rock bottom and fall apart before I die to self and ask for help. But I'm realizing more and more that God doesn't ask us to walk this life alone. Not only has he given us himself, he has given us each other. It helped me to change my perspective when I realized that I am actually robbing Jeff of the opportunity to serve and love me as Christ has called him to when I resist his help out of pride. Of course, that doesn't mean I sit down and do nothing, but it does mean that I need to resist a heart of self-sufficiency and admit when I need help. It can actually fuel intimacy and trust when we allow each other into our weaknesses and sacrificially serve and love the other in that moment. The truth is, we all need to learn to humbly serve, but we also need to humble ourselves to allow others to serve us.

There was a period of time when I battled anger and resentment towards Jeff because it felt unfair that he was healthy and I was always sick. I resented the fact that he could go off to work and leave our stressful and difficult home life whenever he chose to, while I had to bear the weight of it day in and day out, all while not feeling well. For years, that resentment simmered under the surface. But, in God's providence he allowed a season that drew all that was simmering to the surface, beginning a long, painful season of difficult conversations, and what seemed to be a breaking down of our relationship. However, the Lord knew that we needed to be broken down in order to be built back up on a foundation of honesty, trust and sacrificial love for each other.

We had both been solely focused on how our circumstances were affecting us, and responded accordingly. But in the Lord's kindness he drew us to him in our pain and hurt, and in need of his forgiveness, wisdom and healing, and then gradually brought healing and restoration to our relationship. We began to navigate our reality together with greater humility, selflessness and honesty.

Learning a change of perspective

Jeff: I have learned that if I fixate on how hard things are for me and focus on my own wants and needs, rather than the needs of Sarah and our kids, I inevitably become impatient, irritated and discontent – and I dishonour the Lord. But when the Holy Spirit reorients my perspective, I'm reminded that my wife and children are his sons and daughters who he has entrusted to me for a season and are a part of God's good plan for my life. It may not be easy at times, but it's a privilege to lay down my life and serve my family. It's what Christ has called us to as husbands – to walk in his footsteps and lay down our life for our bride, regardless of what the cost may be. But the truth is, I can't do that in my strength. Every day I need to spend time in God's Word and prayer, relying on him to give me the strength to serve and love my family well.

When I'm weary and tired to the point of battling frustration and hopelessness, it's often a sign that I'm leaning on my own strength and understanding. It's all too easy to try to control what feels chaotic and out of control, but it only leads to further stress, anxiety and eventually crashing and burning. In those times, I confess my self-sufficiency and I ask the Lord to give me the strength that I don't have in myself.

I've learned the importance of lament, which brings two worlds together – an honest wrestling with pain and confusion, and a growing trust and renewed hope in the promises of God. I have to give myself permission to grieve the pain and suffering in our lives, but I just can't stay there. I need to bring those disappointments and heartache to Christ and ask him to renew a right spirit in me, remind me of what's true and fill me with a joy and contentment that only he can give. That isn't a one-time process – it's often a daily one. But over time, that process often moves more quickly from grief to truth, and truth to joy.

Our marriage is meant to reflect Christ and his bride, the church. But we often come into marriage focused on our own needs and wants being met, and when they aren't, we begin the crazy cycle of waiting for our spouse to meet our perceived needs before we'll be willing to meet theirs. But this is the opposite of what Christ calls us to as believers. All of marriage, therefore, is a training ground for our hearts to be humbled and shaped into the image of Christ, and learning to sacrificially love and serve our spouse as Christ does the church.

Sarah is a good gift from God, and sex and intimacy are a gift he has given us in the context of marriage. But we can lose sight of what God intended intimacy to be when we fixate on our own needs and desires in that area, elevating our desires or expectations of sex and intimacy above our spouse's. In God's kindness, he has used the extenuating circumstances that have impacted our physical intimacy to open my eyes to see how I was looking to Sarah as the ultimate provider of my needs and joy, rather than the Lord. God gradually opened my eyes to the high calling I have been given to love Sarah sacrificially, expecting nothing in return. Overall, I needed to ask myself if I love Christ above any earthly desire (even good desires), not dependent on what he does or doesn't give me. Over time, Sarah began to trust my love to be genuine, rather than selfishly motivated. That trust fuelled greater intimacy within the whole of our marriage – even when it needed to look different than we initially imagined it would.

Physical intimacy is an amazing gift from God, but it is not the sole purpose of our marriage; it is to be the overflow of the intimacy in the rest of our relationship. When sacrificial love becomes the foundation of our marriage, we stop having expectations and making demands, and we begin to experience the true depth of intimacy that God intended – physically, emotionally and spiritually.

The battle ground of intimacy

Sarah: Yes, intimacy has been one the greatest battle grounds of our marriage. Yet it's also the area that God has brought the most redemption to. We've had everything against us – distorted views of sex after past abuse in my younger years, chronic illness, hormonal problems, a special needs child that consumed my physical and emotional energy, and a husband that was on call 24/7 and often not home. Needless to say, there were no easy answers. For too many years, I went through the motions, fulfilling the role I thought God was calling me to as a wife, but I was slowly dying inside. And as much as Jeff needed to grow in his understanding of intimacy as a whole, I was doing more harm to my marriage by burying my hurt and resentment than if I were to say what was difficult and address things as they really were.

Neither of us knew the answers and neither of us knew a way forward. But, over time, the Lord reached into that dark and hurting place of our marriage and began a deep and long-term work that only he could do. For a season, I needed gospel-centred counsel to help me acknowledge my distorted views of intimacy and to honestly acknowledge the hurt that was so deeply ingrained in me that I could barely recognize its source any more. After that, Jeff and I went through a season of receiving counsel together from a wise and godly counsellor who was able to be a neutral party and help us do the hard work of unpacking the layers of hurt, misunderstandings, fears and distortions. It was incredibly difficult and painful but, for the first time, we were on a path towards genuine healing and growth, rather than a facade of intimacy.

The greatest change came when we stopped looking to the other to satisfy us. We stopped demanding what we thought we were owed and started to ask the Lord to help us love each other sacrificially and experience the joy of serving the other, rather than being served. We still step on each other's toes a lot and we still fall back into old patterns of thinking at times, but we are experiencing a truer, Christ-centred intimacy for the first time in our marriage – one that involves every aspect of our relationship, not just the physical.

Learning to extend God's grace

We have learned how important it is to assume the best in each other. We're often quick to assert motives to each other's actions, rather than being quick to extend grace and assume the best. The more we grasp how little we deserve and how much grace we have been given in Christ, the more we will respond humbly and graciously to each other's struggles. It comes back to understanding the gospel and applying it in those moments. When I was at my worst, Jesus sacrificed himself and died for me in order that I could receive the forgiveness and riches of Christ through faith. In those moments, we are given an opportunity to walk in the footsteps of Christ, laying our own needs and desires aside and sacrificially showing patience, grace and love. In that moment, we are being a reflection of Christ to our spouse, and so often we end up being blessed in the process.

Jeff and Sarah write more about this in their own book Together Through the Storms (*The Good Book Company, 2020*).

Marriage as mission

Claire: We believe that marriage is not just for the couples who are married to one another, but for the community they live within too. As we've said before, when we agree to give our lives to one another, before God, the Scripture that is often cited

Marriage is not just for the couples who are married to one another, but for the community they live within too.

is Ecclesiastes 4:12, which says: 'A cord of three strands is not quickly broken.' This reminds us that we are not only entwined with one another but also with God. He should be at the centre of our marriages, and his will central to all we do.

As married couples, we do not simply please ourselves. But we need to die to ourselves as couples too, as we should be living for God. We are on a mission that we have chosen to go on together, with a purpose that is much bigger than just the two of us to advance his kingdom. This was actually brought home to me during a very odd conversation I was having with my sister after I had left Steve. Her first marriage had broken up a few years previously and she had remarried. I was complaining to her that God kept getting on my case and even said: 'Why won't he just let me walk away, like he let you?' And she said something remarkable, given the struggles and difficulties she had been through. Her quick-as-a-flash response was: 'Because he has a bigger plan for your marriage.' I didn't like hearing that then, but I still remember it to this day.

While I don't believe God favours one marriage over another (and Steve has already indicated how much he was fighting for ours), I have come to believe that God does have plans and purposes for our marriages that are way bigger than ourselves and what we might envisage. The way we have seen our ministry reaching to those with marital difficulties or anyone (single or married) who simply needs the 'permission' to be vulnerable has shown us this very vividly. But there is a cost to that too.

As a shy introvert, I would never have chosen to write and then speak about the most sin-filled, painful part of my life. And as I explained in *Taking Off the Mask*, Steve is an extremely private person, so for him to agree that God was indeed calling me to enter this new season with my writing and speaking was costly for him as well. Particularly as it has birthed this book too, in which he is directly involved! But each time I think, 'What on earth am I doing?' and get overwhelmed by how vulnerable I have made myself to strangers, I immediately feel confirmation in my heart that when I lay down my pride and am honest about my failings and how God has redeemed me, he *will* use it for his kingdom purposes. As Jesus said in Matthew 16: 'whoever wants to save their life will lose it, but whoever loses their life for me will find it' (v.25).

When Steve became an elder at our church, giving up record producing completely, I'm sure some felt I should be over the moon. No longer would he be working around the clock. But all I could think of was the fact that he would be on call 24/7 in the eyes of the congregation. I was also worried about what they might expect of me. I was battling a bout of depression, had a young child, and was also wrestling with some rebellion and sin. I didn't want to pay the price I knew this new calling would involve. Even though Steve and I had been a part of the small group of people who had committed to start this church, and even though they had stuck by us throughout our difficulties and welcomed me back after I came home, I still recoiled from this frightening challenge. I hadn't signed up to be married to a pastor. I didn't know what it might mean for me, and I didn't like the fact I might have to explore something different.

There are times when I still struggle, as I know I'm not called to work for the church full time like Steve is, and I believe my writing, speaking and editing is very much part of my calling. That became clear to me when Steve first took over the church as lead pastor. There were no other members of staff and so Steve was doing everything that has to be done in a church office. He would be the first to say organizational skills are not his strong point, and so I really wrestled with whether I should give up my job and become his PA. After a few days pondering and praying, I answered that with a resounding 'No!' Yet I *do* believe that God has called me to stand side by side with Steve and model loving vulnerability at the front of our church, week in, week out. Sometimes that is incredibly painful and costly, when I'm working through some exceedingly personal issues and God nudges me to share and encourage others to come openly and vulnerably before him. Part of me screams inwardly, 'Not again! Please just leave me alone,' while the rest of me calmly ignores that bit and walks forward to pick up the microphone and start sharing. Because I recognize that that is an integral part of the dying to self that God has asked me to do personally.

We hope that we are sharing this idea of being on mission together with our children too, as it isn't simply about us and they *have* to tag along because their dad works for the church and their mum is often playing in the worship team. We know that, practically, it will feel like that for them at times, but we also know that they are deepening friendships and learning to talk about their faith with their peers. And what they do on a Sunday flows out into who they are in their schools during the week.

There is certainly a battle, both within our marriage and also in our family. When Steve is preaching and especially on those Sunday mornings when I'm leading worship too, the dynamics in our family can feel quite volatile. The spiritual pressure certainly goes up a notch. But in those moments when our kids moan about having to get to church early, being there late or having people over when they'd rather just chill out as a family, we try and gently remind them that we feel our lives are built around the calling to be a wider community with those in our church and beyond. Our deep desire is for them to buy into it too, as we are on mission together as a family. We see it in glimpses, such as the time our daughter was talking enthusiastically about a youth camp and one of her (Hindu) friends ended up going along with her. The way she naturally intermingles faith with other conversation is actually a provocation to me . . .

> Our lives are built around the calling to be a wider community with those in our church and beyond.

I was challenged afresh at a conference recently, where the issue of whether our church is inclusive or not was being discussed. The speakers were talking about how marriage can be set up as the ideal, and how those who aren't married, who don't have children, etc. can feel like second-class citizens within the local church. We were encouraged to think about the fact that family doesn't just mean our biological family. These days, with families being dotted around the world, often it is the church family that we see most and who help us with practical challenges day to day. As married couples, as families, are we reflecting this reality by being open-hearted and inclusive of others?

I started thinking about the fact that, when we were fully back on board with our church but before we had children, we were opening our home regularly each week on week nights for small group meetings, prayer meetings and worship meetings, plus having people round for meals at the weekends. But it was also a place where both couples and singles felt comfortable inviting themselves round. That did continue when our kids were really little, but I was struck by how it seems to have happened less since they became a tween and a teenager. Naturally, there are some seasons when it is easier to open your home regularly, but we did end up talking to our children about how we want to extend more of an open invitation to people again. We also discussed what riches we gain through various different types of friendships, including with singles who may not have other expressions of family to enjoy, and inter-generational, which provides our kids with wisdom from those older than ourselves.

Open hearts and an open home

Writer and blogger Lucy Rycroft reflects on how her marriage has always been about reaching out to those around them – through hospitality, adoption and general church and home life.

One of the things I find so fascinating about marriage is the coming together of two different family cultures. I love watching how two families become one, as a newly married couple work out how they're going to set up their household, taking influences from both families but also doing something completely new.

Forging the way

Both of us have come from Christian families who are extremely hospitable, but in very different ways: one family gives elaborate and extravagant hospitality, while the other opens its doors to anybody and everybody. So right from the outset we knew we wanted to have an open home, taking the best of what we'd seen from our families, but forging our own path too.

In our early, child-free years of marriage, hospitality was about hosting others for meals, parties, small group socials, youth groups and so on. When Al was training for ordination, on placement in a church with lots of students, we were able to welcome lots of them to our home for meals and chats. One even came for a few nights' sleep during stressful finals; he is still a close friend to this day.

The danger, of course, in 'dying to self' within a marriage is that you become so focused on others' needs that you forget your commitment to each other. On one occasion, I offered short-term accommodation to quite a difficult colleague and her 12-year-old son when her marriage turned sour. It's testament to my husband's character that he welcomed them in, but we had good friends visiting from overseas during that period, and our house was fairly small, so they had to sleep in our lounge. To say the situation wasn't ideal is an understatement.

I learned then that, after God, my first priority is to my husband. We might try and kid ourselves that we 'need' to provide for this person or that person, but the truth is that God is the one who provides. He may graciously use our marriage to do this, but when we can't meet a need we can see, we mustn't feel guilty, as he will provide another way.

Adjusting to family life

When we moved to Al's curacy post and started having children, our hospitality changed as we realized (again, through making mistakes) that our family had to take priority. We were often too tired in the evenings to invite people over for dinner, but started instead to have more people round for Sunday lunch or Saturday brunch. Through the week, I had loads of friends and their children round for play dates. Our home has always been a place where our children know their friends are welcome.

Nine years into marriage – with a 2-year-old and a newborn baby – God started to tug at our heart-strings about adoption. It was something that had unnerved me in previous years, but I now found myself starting to become excited about it. God spoke to Al about adoption too, totally independently.

Before that was to happen, though, God would bring several friends to live with us at different points: some just for a few days, the longest for two years. Again, these opportunities to offer hospitality taught us so much about the capacity for our marriage and home to become a safe haven for others. Even when we were exhausted with caring for our two small children and – for my husband – working full-time, God was more than able to take what we had (a good-sized vicarage) and use it to bless others for his glory.

Finally, when our birth children were 6 and 4, God's call on us to adopt was realized, and we welcomed beautiful 1-year-old twin boys into our family.

Adoption is just another form of hospitality, really. It is offering back to God what he has given us – in our case, a strong marriage, emotionally resilient birth children and extra bedrooms. Just like the boy with his five loaves and two fishes, God multiplies what we have when we give it to him! Adoption and hospitality are, essentially, a way of handing over control to God and allowing him to shape our families how he will, rather than storming ahead with our own ideas of what our marriage and family life will look like.

Getting the balance

Our family doesn't look conventional. Besides having four children within a five-year age gap, we are dealing with the effects of early life trauma on a daily basis. We have more tantrums and emotional outbursts than the average family – and the underlying shame behind these sometimes seems impossible to shift.

Our family doesn't conform to what other families may or may not be doing in terms of days out, activities or discipline: we've had to, once again, find our own way. However, we haven't been alone; God has stayed close every step of the way, guiding and encouraging us, and giving us so much joy as an imperfect family. We are so close to each other and to our children, and I believe this gives us a great base for being able to extend a hospitable arm to others.

Our children regularly invite friends round, and sometimes we have the whole family over for a meal. Sunday lunch with different members of our church family has become a bit of a tradition – in fact, our children are disappointed when it doesn't happen!

But our hospitality also has limits, imposed by our family. We recently separated our older two children into different bedrooms, meaning we no longer have a spare room. I was disappointed at first that we would be unable to build an extra bedroom, but the more I thought about it, the more I felt God's peace. I felt he was saying, 'This is the time to focus on your family; overnight guests will be less of a priority.'

God is so gracious. When we see our marriages as a starting point for mission and outreach, he really does look after us and protects us. I feel a huge burden has been lifted in terms of accommodating friends and family when they come to visit. When my family came to celebrate a recent New Year with us, they were able to stay in the house of my friend, whose family were away. Her generous hospitality aided ours. When we work together as a community of people who love Jesus, we are stronger.

Our home is also my husband's workspace. We both feel, in keeping with our desire to be hospitable, that we want others to feel at home when they come to visit us. But it has also been important to set some boundaries. Fortunately, we don't live in the sort of parish where people just barge in without knocking! But still, we protect my husband's day off and our 'marriage night' together, and we protect the upstairs so our children can have their own space.

It might be tempting – and more intuitive – to protect our marriages and families by closing ourselves off to others. I'm not suggesting there aren't seasons when we might need to do this for a short period. But, for the most part, we need community around us. In blessing others, we ourselves are blessed. This might be a direct blessing, like inviting some students over for lunch and finding that they're awesome at entertaining your children for you. Or it might be longer term: some of the closest friendships we enjoy outside our immediate family unit have been built through our hospitality.

I do want to end by emphasizing again that we must set healthy boundaries for our marriages. We must invest in them regularly by spending time together and having deep conversations (not just whose turn it is to put the bin out!). When we do this, we will find that God uses our strong relationships to bless the wider community, drawing others close to him in the process. It is an exciting journey!

Lucy shares regular articles and other resources on adoption, faith and family life at: https://thehopefilledfamily.com.

Over to you

- Have you ever thought of your marriage as a means of dying to yourself?
- Try making a concerted effort one day this week to show your partner in some practical way how you are dying to your own needs and wants so that you can put theirs first.
- In what ways are you on mission together in your marriage? Are you feeling stirred to reach out in a new way?

Grace Champions the Other

Be devoted to one another in love. Honour one another above yourselves.

Romans 12:10

There is a myth rife that we need to find our perfect partner who is simply out there waiting for us, as we will only be 'complete' when we have. This is often emphasized in fairy tales and romantic comedies, but also underlies a lot of marketing. It is such an unhelpful myth, and can cause those who aren't in a 'perfect' marriage to feel that perhaps they made a mistake, and those who are single to feel like lesser people. The truth is we are *only* complete in Jesus. I am sure you have already discovered this, but we aren't a 'half person' waiting for the other half to make us into a 'whole'. We are our own people, with our own callings from God on our lives and we find our wholeness in him. In marriage we get to team with another person – and often they do back us up by being strong in areas that we are weak (isn't that great – it's wonderful to see God's wisdom in that). Marriage also isn't about one person having to give up their calling in order to help the other fulfil theirs; it's about spurring one another on to be all that God has designed us to be.

Claire: As you will have picked up, the early stages of our marriage were difficult. With Steve working around the clock, I got involved in many things within our church that he couldn't, and continued with my career. However, I felt I was doing those things alone and, at times, I got very resentful. It felt I was married but with none of the benefits; I often felt like a single person. But, as we settled into married life once Steve was around a lot more, we began to realize that we could support each other well (and even plan and run things together, which we particularly enjoy doing). As we have said, God has called us to run things like marriage preparation classes together, and there is much in church leadership that we do together too. Of course, writing this book together is a way that we are spearheading something new in our joint ministry.

But we are also both involved in various other areas of ministry and work separately, and need the support of the other in the background, particularly with our family. We talk about what is coming up, and ensure that the person we feel has a particular calling for that moment can concentrate on it. Practically, this means I am often at home with our children while Steve runs church-based evening events. As the worship team leader, I usually talk over the new songs that I'm planning to introduce with Steve, as I value his input (as my husband but also as our church leader). When I'm running an event or a music practice, he often comes and helps me to set up. At other times, he takes over my usual roles around the home so that I can travel away to speak at an event elsewhere.

> It is so worth all the conversations and tweaking that we need to do to our schedules in order to accommodate what each of us feels called to do.

There are times when this is more challenging than others, but it is so worth all the conversations and tweaking that we need to do to our schedules in order to accommodate what each of us feels called to do. In fact, those practical necessities help us to keep communicating about what we are doing, and it gives us the opportunity to pray for one another too.

The dance of preferring one another

Katia and Julian Adams are the founding directors of charity Frequentsee, which seeks to empower men and women to really reach their potential in Christ, and to bring the kingdom of God into their spheres of influence (http//:www.frequentsee.org). They are currently church planting together in Boston, Massachusetts. Here they share about how they have learned to navigate life in a way that means they are constantly shifting in order to champion one another.

We have tried to model our marriage out of the conviction that the Trinity works to prefer and make room for one another. The beautiful dance of the Father, Son and Holy Spirit, how they move around one another and allow one to represent the whole in different moments, is what we want to echo, and what we believe the Bible invites us into as we're encouraged to 'submit to one another' (Eph. 5:21). Throughout the Bible, you see these snapshots of Father, Son and Spirit putting the spotlight on one another and so we have tried to be intentional about making this a reality in our marriage.

Katia: Practically, this means that when we can sense a particular season of favour upon one of us, the other does all they can to make room for them to shine. This can mean that one needs to step back from what they are doing in order to allow the other to move forward. For instance, when I was researching and then writing my book *Equal*, Julian took on a lot of the administration and practical work around the home in order to give me space and time to do so. As we are both preachers, sometimes one of us stays home to look after the children while the other travels, or you might find one of us at the back of an auditorium caring for our babies while cheering the other who is preaching at the front. At times, if one of us is asked to speak and yet we know the other is more gifted in the subject at that point, we put their name forward, championing them over ourselves.

An ever-changing dance

We have seen our dance change and develop over the years. When we were first married, I was the one who organized and looked after our finances, as we both recognized I had more capacity for that particular role. Having had two children, my head for numbers is not what it once was, and so I am grateful that Julian has taken up leadership of this area of our lives.

Julian: Katia is usually the one who is most ready to embrace high-risk moments, encouraging us both to do so, whereas I tend to be the one who takes a step back, to look at our family as a whole and to weigh up what faith-filled wisdom looks like. If one of us was to permanently take the lead on faith decisions we would likely end up in dangerous territory. The dance of preferring one another and walking in submission allows us to marry risk-taking with faith-filled wisdom.

This kind of a marriage is perhaps not the easiest or simplest to practise. If you have pre-defined roles, and one always takes the lead and the other always follows, then there is a much more structured, clear-cut approach to life. A lot of complexity is eliminated by assigning rigid roles. But we've become convinced that the complexity – and mystery – of two lives intertwined in full equality is the most beautiful expression of God joining a man and woman to be one. While this requires quite a lot more juggling and decision-making, we are thrilled to be living such a rich adventure in the journey of mutual submission. We love how this reflects the mystery and beauty that God has created within marriage.

Day-to-day encouragement

While we recognize there are particular seasons in which we need to consciously champion one of us – focusing on their ministry for that moment – we could all do with more encouragement regularly. Life is tough, and to know our partner is standing with us, and visibly and verbally showing us how much they are supporting us, is so helpful. We have already talked about words of affirmation (see Chapter 5), but we do all need the encouragement each day to keep going, to press in and persevere. The Bible recognizes this – we love *The Message* translation of 1 Thessalonians 5:11: 'So speak encouraging words to one another. Build up hope so you'll all be together in this, no one left out, no one left behind.' While this is a general verse, it can apply so well to marriage too. We need to help each other build up our levels of hope and expectation, to ensure that neither of us gets left behind.

Claire: One of the ways I am having to learn this is by curbing my natural tendency to nag. I get very frustrated when there is a lot to do around the home and I have asked for help but Steve isn't very quick at doing it, or forgets to pick something up or put it away once he's used it. As words of affirmation are so important to him, words of negativity in the form of nagging hit home really hard.

Steve: I do need lots of verbal affirmation. And when I find the opposite happening I can feel my heart harden up and my ears become closed to what is actually being said which, most of the time, has a lot of truth in it. In fact, I even annoy myself in the way I don't put things back after I have used them! However, instead of responding helpfully, I can find myself actively rebelling against what Claire is pointing out. I may even, at times, quote passages like Proverbs 27:15: 'A quarrelsome [nagging] wife is like the dripping of a leaky roof in a rainstorm'. (Hint: quoting Scripture like this is never a good strategy!) If we are not careful, a mudslinging match can unfold. We have been told so many times that words of encouragement get better results than those full of nagging. And it really is true – we just recognize this as an area where we could both learn to champion the other more.

Claire: Sometimes our encouragement best comes in the form of a reminder to our partner of the truth of God's Word. There is so much richness, and goodness, for our lives today, as Paul explains: 'For everything that was written in the past was written to teach us, so that through the endurance taught in the Scriptures and the encouragement they provide we might have hope' (Rom. 15:4). When one of us is finding it hard to focus on the truth, the other can remind them (graciously of course!) of what God's Word says – about God, about them and about whatever situation they find themselves in. As long as it is done in the right way at the right time of course (see the section on championing in the difficult times, below).

It is also true that we can be good at being intentional about encouraging other people, but often forget the person closest to us. Do you remember, for example, to thank your partner when they do or say something that really blesses you? Or has it become so much a part of life that you expect it and therefore don't really think about the need to thank them? If we want to cultivate a culture of championing one another, starting with the small things can really help.

Another small but really significant way we can champion one another is taking the time to celebrate the little 'wins' in everyday life. Perhaps your partner has just finished a project at work and their boss has told them they are pleased with what they've done. Do you celebrate that at home? Depending on what your partner's love language is (see Chapter 5), you could arrange a way to mark that in however small or large a way you want (perhaps writing them a card, taking them for a meal out, buying them some flowers, cooking them a nice meal, having a movie night together – whatever it is you know would mean the most to them). And before those 'wins' have happened, how do you intentionally champion one another in the midst of the process? Taking time to talk over your days, vocalize the challenges you each face (again see Chapter 5) and pray together can really help solidify your sense of togetherness. Thinking about projects that you have coming up, and the sorts of questions you would want your partner to ask you about them (including, 'How can I help so that you can carve out more time for this?') can really help you to consider what you might need to ask your spouse about the things *they* are currently involved in.

Championing your partner in front of others

To champion someone means to vigorously support or defend them. The noun is obviously describing someone who has come out on top, defeating all those around them and, interestingly, the origins of the word 'champion' come from various places (including Middle English, Old French and Medieval Latin), describing a fighter. Putting this all together, we see that championing our partner is about more than simply saying nice things to them in the comfort of our own home, or organizing our schedules so that they can do the things they feel called to. It's also about sticking up for them in front of other people, and highlighting what we love about them and particular current achievements in the presence of others too.

For far too long, I'm ashamed to say, I actually seemed to enjoy putting Steve down in front of others. I don't know if it was the resentment and rejection bubbling up from underneath the surface, or simply my natural bent towards sarcasm, but I used to take the opportunity when we were with others to engage in what I viewed as 'banter'. Often it was quite light-hearted, but sometimes it did end up with me having a right old moan about him in front of other people. Now there is a time and place for us to involve others when we need to communicate about difficulties in our marriage, but that was not what I was doing at all. There was no intentionality about it and I was just doing it to vent rather than for any constructive purpose. I didn't ever stop to consider how it made Steve feel, as I was so wrapped up in my own bubble of emotions. Taking time to recognize this has made me understand how easily I can slip into the sort of language or behaviour that isn't helpful or honouring of my partner.

Learning to cherish each other

Scripturally, we are taught over and over again to love one another (there are over 50 'one anothering' verses in the Bible[1]). While they are usually written in the context of general discipleship with other believers, it is important not to neglect the same principles with our marriage partners! Romans 12:10 is really helpful, and challenging, for our marriage: 'Be devoted to one another in love. Honour one another above yourselves.' One of the ways we show our devotion to our spouse is not just by loving them, but by honouring them above ourselves. That means respecting and holding them in higher esteem than ourselves. When we are in the first flushes of romantic love, it can seem that this will be easy to do throughout our lives. However, when that dies down, when life is pretty mundane, or challenging even, choosing to honour can be costly.

Honouring and cherishing are closely related. Not only are we to show how much we respect our partners, but we are also called to 'hold [them] dear',[2] to want to protect and care for them. Gary Thomas unpacks this in great detail in his book *Cherish*,[3] in which he points out that cherishing means we want to showcase that which we hold dear; we want to treat with tenderness what or who we cherish. He explains that love is about meeting one another's needs and nurturing each other, while cherishing is being enthralled by our partner and wanting to celebrate them. What he is at pains to point out is how cherishing (as well as loving) is a choice, but when we cherish, we also learn to delight in our partners.

I was really taken aback when I read that for the first time. Life has been pretty hard recently, and I know that Steve is totally for me and has supported me practically day by day.

We have also gone deeper in our prayer life together as we have done battle for issues our family has been facing. But as I look back over the last few months, could I say that I feel cherished? Not so much. And, if I was being honest with myself, would Steve say the same thing? I concluded that he wasn't feeling too cherished either.

I was even more intrigued to read about the link between cherishing and delighting. I pray for one word to focus on in my walk with God each year, and 'delight' was the word God gave me for this year. I had already been delving into how I could delight more in God, and also receive the affirmation of how much he delights in me. I had even started to think about how I could show my children more of the delight I find in them. But I hadn't applied the same word to my marriage! As I began to delve more deeply into what cherishing Steve may mean, I found some really positive things – but also some big challenges.

For example, I read in Gary's book about how some couples have learned to be so in step with one another that they antici-pate one another's needs. This has happened to us, but not that often. However, I immediately thought of how often we are thinking exactly the same thing, say the same thing at the same time or come to the same conclusion about what we should do about a situation. There is much that we feel 'in tune' about; it's time to take that to the next level.

Learning to cherish our partner involves a change in per-spective and approach. It's about thinking about the other first, considering ways we can showcase them rather than ourselves. Ways that we can ensure they flourish. That's why we wanted to include Katia and Julian's story in this chapter; because they are working together in ministry they have found a way to help one another 'step forward' when they believe it is their time, which means the other partner has to get very practical, often staying behind to look after their kids and home.

Taking a step back and even intentionally pushing our partner forward can seem quite alien. We can be so selfish naturally, that it can be hard to change our mindset to think like this first and foremost, but if we don't, we end up focusing on ourselves more than our partners, and that causes distance between us. The wonderful thing is, when we do cherish our partners, our marriages and our own wellbeing will be enriched too. We know it is hard to think that we can ever get to this point, particularly when we have been hurt by our partner, but alongside repentance and forgiveness (see Chapter 4), intentionally cherishing one another makes a huge difference to what is, essentially, a lifelong commitment between two imperfect humans. We will still do things that annoy and upset our partner and vice versa, but if those are the things we focus on, our sense of bitterness and anger will increase. How often do we go out of our way to notice and comment on the things we love about our partner, and the things they do that make our lives easier?[4]

I would always assume that I was going to be let down, and that so easily leads to feeling bitterness and contempt towards your partner. Just as we learned in the conflict chapter never to say 'You always . . .' (see Chapter 7), so too we need to keep a check on our thoughts to ensure they aren't going down the same route (such as thinking: 'I bet I'm going to find all his clothes all over the floor yet again, as he never bothers to pick them up.'). Instead of focusing on the imperfections that there are within our partner, cherishing means choosing to celebrate their gifts and helping them to

> Cherishing means choosing to celebrate their gifts and helping them to develop those.

develop those. I'm sure we would all prefer that our partners did that for us and so, rather than thinking about the negative impact their faults may make to our lives, and rather than focusing on what we want, we look to see how we can elevate our partner and give them pleasure. Incredibly, when we do this, our own sense of joy increases.

Cherishing means fixing our eyes on the positives along the way, and ignoring what might be personal niggles. For example, Steve has taken to doing more cooking of evening meals, now that he often works from home. It helps ease the pressure of me having to think of something to cook each day and also juggle finishing off work, as well as interacting with the children after school. However, he is a very messy cook, who doesn't like to tidy up after himself straight away. I have to admit that I can often enter the kitchen, stressed and rushing, and not notice the fact that a wonderful pie is cooking in the oven – I just see the mess and think about the extra work it could mean. But when I comment on the mess, rather than curbing my tongue (or thanking him for the delicious smell emanating from the oven), it makes Steve less likely to want to cook again.

Steve: I think a mistake we men often make is assuming that it is just our wives who long to be cherished. We can think about it more in terms of being romantically pursued and treasured and, while that is extremely important, the truth is we all need to be cherished in little ways throughout the day. So often we can be rushing about getting all our daily tasks done, or mingling with other people if we are in a social setting. How often do we stop to make a connection with our partner during the course of the day? We live in an age where we can be continually distracted by other things vying for our affections. It may sound obvious but we do need to guard what we look at and what we give our attention to. For example, if you spend most of your time at home with your face in your phone, looking at your social media feeds, what message is that sending to your partner? To cherish means to have your focus, your gaze fixed on the one you desire. That means not just spending time in the same room but time really connecting.

We made a conscious decision to watch TV programmes together, even if one of us wouldn't choose a particular programme for ourselves. However, I have noticed, while sitting next to Claire during an episode of *Call the Midwife* (for example), how often my hand reaches for my phone! And when we are having a conversation, how often do we prioritize an incoming text over what our partner is trying to say? I know that one of the biggest ways Claire can feel unnoticed, and not cherished is when she is trying to communicate with me and/or the kids, and not one of us lifts our eyes up from whatever device we are on.

What we look at and prioritize speaks volumes to our partner about how we are cherishing them. That includes what we spend time looking at on our own. Spending all our time looking at people's picture perfect, edited lives on social media will leave us comparing what we have – and discontentment can so quickly follow. Pornography also falls squarely into this category. You will struggle to cherish your partner if you are looking at porn. Not only are you dishonouring them and God (see Heb. 13:4), it is also modelling an objectifying, self-centredness that is quite the opposite to cherishing and rejoicing in the wife of your youth (Prov. 5:18). (See Chapter 8 for more on this.)

Cherishing may sound like it takes a lot of work – just like loving, it *is* a verb, and yes, we need to be intentional, but, actually, the return we get for our efforts makes it well worth it.

Championing one another in the hardest of times

Claire: There are times when life seems bleak, when we feel we are wading through treacle and the very thought of trying to actively find delight in one another seems almost laughable. Those heart-rending moments of deep loss, pain and disappointment are inevitable for us all (as Jesus said: 'In this world you will have trouble,' John 16:33). How do we keep from closing in on ourselves and protecting our hearts from more pain by shutting down?

I think when we truly learn on a heart level that our saviour was a suffering servant, that he faced temptation, despair, ridicule, rejection and the darkest separation, we can begin to open up to him, trusting that he does indeed understand. For each of us, our journeys with suffering will be unique, and so trotting out verses and writing down platitudes seems somewhat trite. And yet, having lived through a recent time of wrestling deeply with confusing questions and darkness I can say that, however hopeless I felt at times, I always knew God was by my side (which sometimes seemed counter-intuitive, given what I was wrestling with). Knowing that helped me to respond to Steve when he reached out to me, and helped me to try and explain some of what I was dealing with (I didn't always get that right). And when we faced a really difficult issue as a family, we found that we clung to Jesus together. While we prayed and sought God separately, there was so much more praying and petitioning God together. We literally and figuratively clung on to each other as we clung on to God.

Sometimes our championing of our spouse will simply be praying for them, seeking to alleviate physical needs by anticipating and fulfilling them but also reminding them of the truth of God's Word. In the final part of John 16:33, Jesus says: 'But take heart! I have overcome the world.' At times we need to be reminded by our partner of the everlasting truth that we have a living hope even in the midst of such darkness. Of course, there are moments when being told that wouldn't be helpful at all. I am reminded of how Job's friends simply sat in silence with him when they first heard about all of his losses. It can be so powerful when we do that for our spouse (see Job 2:11–13). But then Job's friends

> At times we need to be reminded by our partner of the everlasting truth that we have a living hope even in the midst of such darkness.

got a bit frustrated, felt the need to work out an explanation, and decided to tell Job what they thought. They may have sincerely felt they were speaking truths about God and who he is (see Job 8 for instance), but they made wrong assumptions about both him and Job, which God was angered by (see Job 42:7–9). We need to ask God for his wisdom when we are seeking to care and champion our partner in a particularly painful season, as his Holy Spirit can guide us as to when to speak and when to simply hold them. When to be present, and when they need space (see Chapter 6 for more on giving space to one another).

'We've decided we won't let IVF come between us'

Originally from Australia, Sheridan and Merryn Voysey are a couple that have chosen to keep cherishing one another even in the midst of deep sorrow. Sheridan here describes the intense pain of discovering infertility and the resulting emotionally exhausting journey, and how, even in the midst of their shattered dreams, he and his wife Merryn determined to champion one another, putting each other first in whatever they faced in life.

Merryn and I married in December of 1996. By the year 2000 we felt ready to start a family. While we weren't intentionally 'trying', any couple who has made the decision to come off contraception is naturally expectant as each month rolls round. The first few months we weren't too concerned – it can take some time to conceive. But after nine months without success we got some tests done, which revealed there was a significant problem on my side with both sperm count and quality, and that, barring technological assistance or a divine miracle, conception was going to be near impossible for us.

Those test results marked the start of a decade-long journey for us, with seasons of trying to rectify our situation interspersed with periods of putting the problem aside. We tried special diets and supplements, and even chiropractic (for the life of me, I have no idea why). We tried healing prayer numerous times. In 2006 we did our first round of IVF (ICSI), without success. In 2007 we began exploring adoption, beginning a lengthy assessment process that resulted in us being added to the 'waiting' list of couples ready to adopt. By 2010 – ten years after our decision to start a family – no adoption had happened with no reasons known. With Merryn now in an emotional mess from the waiting, we made the difficult decision to halt our adoption journey to do more IVF (in the New South Wales system in Australia, as in the UK, you can't stay in the adoption pool while also doing IVF). We set out to do as many rounds of IVF as it would take to get our baby. By December 2010, exhausted from a number of unsuccessful rounds, we had one embryo left for transfer. We decided this was our last try. We'd given ten years to the dream, tried everything we felt ethically comfortable doing, and would move on as a childless couple if this last embryo didn't result in a pregnancy.

The embryo was transferred. And to everyone's surprise, a nurse from the IVF clinic called with news we'd given up ever hearing – we were pregnant. While we were too exhausted to celebrate just yet, and still a little wary of it being true, jubilation erupted amongst our friends and family. Then on Christmas Eve we got another call from the clinic. It turned out the IVF drugs had created a gestational sac – a sac that should have held a baby, but there wasn't one there. Even the doctors had been fooled. Merryn put the phone down, walked into our bedroom and curled up on the bed in a foetal position. Our journey to parenthood was over.

Expectation then disappointment . . . again and again

Proverbs 13:12 says that hope deferred 'makes the heart sick'. The infertile couple soon discovers just how true this is. At first, when you're trying for a child, you're waiting every 28 days, hoping a period is missed. Then when you're doing IVF, you're waiting for blood test results after a transfer. When you get accepted as potential adoptive parents, you're waiting for the phone call telling you to come and collect your child – a call that could come any day, influencing when and if you take holidays, whether you should go for a job opportunity, make a cross-country move, and affecting other life decisions. Your emotions get a battering during each of these waits, as your hopes are constantly raised then dashed. And when your expectation is regularly met with disappointment *for years* . . . it has a cumulative effect that leaves you exhausted, jaded and deeply sad. You even start feeling fearful of your expectations being raised again because of the inevitable crash that will follow. This affects your spiritual life too. Expectation is a good response to prayer but when the prayers consistently go unanswered, you don't want to pray or have anyone pray for you any more because of the crash that may follow.

Facing big questions about the future

In addition, infertile couples find themselves asking many questions about their lives and futures. In my book *Resurrection Year*, I include some of the ones we were wrestling with: What are we to be? Who will we become? Will we forever feel sad as we walk past a playground, with its parents and toddlers and games of tag? Will we feel isolated and envious as friends start their families, and will we lose touch as we live different lives? Will we feel lonely in our 40s, with our careers in full swing but with awards on the walls instead of drawings? And when old age hits, who will help us get dressed? Take us on outings? Listen to our mutterings?

Notice how all those fears are written in the future tense – *Will we forever feel sad walking past a playground? Will we feel lonely in our 40s?* Looking back now, I see that we could only answer those questions by reaching those points. By the end of *Resurrection Year* readers find us celebrating our 40th birthdays and *not* being lonely. Merryn and I can walk past a playground today and not be gripped with sadness. So, much of what we fear is simply wasted emotional energy. I have to remind myself of that with some of the other questions in that passage – *When old age hits, who will help us get dressed? Take us on outings?* Those are real questions for us still, ones we can plan for to some degree, but will only fully answer when we arrive at that stage of life. This is where faith really does come in. We trust God, and prepare as wisely for that life stage as we can.

Dealing with our disappointment . . . in different ways

There are two common responses to long-term unanswered prayer. One is to shake our fists at heaven, wondering why God isn't acting. The other is to point fingers at ourselves, wondering if our lack of faith or some other sin is to blame. Merryn took the first option, I took the second.

Our ten years of disappointment raised some very real and natural questions about God's goodness for Merryn. Why would abusive parents be given a child and good ones not? What could you really trust God for when your prayers were seemingly ignored for so long? Was God really good or, in fact, mean? Biblically, Merryn was in good company with such questions, with Job, Habakkuk and the Israelites during their wilderness wanderings asking the same questions. It took time for her to work them through, and I had to be careful not to preach at her or push her to answers she wasn't ready for.

For me, the problem couldn't be God. God is perfect, all his ways are just, and I had enough evidence in the beauty of the world to believe he wasn't mean. So to my mind, if there was a problem, it must be with me. Maybe I didn't have enough faith for a healing. Maybe I wasn't Spirit-filled enough. These questions tore me apart at times, especially towards the end of our journey when I was often holding a weeping wife after yet more bad news, feeling responsible for her not getting what she desperately wanted. I had to come to peace with the fact I couldn't have prayed or believed more than I had, and the reason for our childlessness being either God's will for a greater cause, or simply a mystery.

In all this I'm grateful that Merryn and I have always been able to discuss our feelings, even if at times we didn't know quite what it was we were feeling in the moment. That happened to me on numerous occasions, and in just talking it through – 'I don't know what I'm feeling right now. Is it anger? Is it grief? Maybe it's a bit of both . . .' – I'd be able to find the emotion and express it. Sometimes Merryn would experience something similar. There was much sitting together on couches and walking in parks talking things through and listening. And we both had to allow each other to walk our unique paths processing our disappointment, not pushing the other to be where we wanted them to be.

Holding to our core commitment

I'll never forget Merryn and me talking with an IVF counsellor back in 2003. 'In-vitro fertilization can strain a relationship,' the counsellor said. 'You'll have many decisions to make, like how many rounds of IVF you'll attempt and what you'll do if you don't succeed. Some couples find this the most difficult part. It can lead to many disagreements.' Merryn said, 'Sheridan and I have talked about that, and we've decided we won't let IVF come between us. Our marriage is more important than having a child.' The counsellor slumped with relief and said, 'I'm so glad to hear you say that. Only last week a woman told me in front of her husband that if she didn't have a baby their marriage was over.'

The pressure of infertility on a couple can be immense, whatever route the couple takes to rectify it. But that commitment to put our marriage first made all the difference in surviving those pressures. We made that decision quite early in our journey, before things got more and more emotionally intense. Maybe there's a grace in that – the decision was made before the real emotional stress came. For us it was never questioned though. As difficult as things got, as much as we may have argued, our core commitment was never in question. I'm glad about that.

Grieving the old, grasping the new

Proverbs 13:12 captured our experience so well: hope deferred really does make the heart sick. But the verse continues: 'but a longing fulfilled is a tree of life'. With the dream of motherhood off the table, it was time for Merryn to have a consolation prize.

The only other thing she'd wanted to do with her life was live and work overseas, so when she was offered a job at the University of Oxford, we saw that as God's provision for her.

It was important for us to grieve properly before we moved, though, as it's easy for a new opportunity to become an excuse to run from a problem. There were two things for us to grieve. The first, obviously, was not having a child. Unlike other losses – the death of a loved one, the loss of a job, the lack of children through menopause or a hysterectomy – there is no clearly marked end with infertility. You could keep 'trying', keep doing IVF, keep waiting for the adoption agency's phone call. So you have to make your own ending, draw your own line in the sand. We did that by making our last embryo the 'end'. Whatever happened beyond its transfer, we wouldn't pursue any further treatment. That allowed us to grieve when the result was negative.

The second thing to grieve was my work in Australia. Professionally, things were going well for me there, with a national radio show, book contracts and good speaking engagements. In my line of work 'platform' is key, and by leaving Australia for England I would be pressing reset on my profession. And that's largely what happened, with British publishers at first turning me down because I wasn't known to readers, and the BBC originally ignoring my calls. Thankfully, things have since turned around, but the first two years were full of a deep loss of identity and a confusion of purpose. While the work I now do reaches far more people than before, I sometimes wonder if I've finished grieving the loss of that Australian radio show. I find myself sad whenever I think about it. Sometimes grief takes time.

Our move to the UK has proven to be brilliant for Merryn. She came to the best university in the world for her field of vaccinology, and has only risen in responsibility and expertise since – to the point of becoming the senior statistician for the Oxford Covid-19 vaccine trial. A job is no replacement for a child, of course, but Oxford really was the new beginning she needed. And while things have come good for me, I think our marriage could have suffered in these early years of relocation, when things were more difficult for me. I think the reason it didn't comes down to two things:

Firstly, I made a commitment to myself that I wouldn't remind Merryn of the 'sacrifice' I'd made for her. That would be easy to do as time went on, maybe during some fight or other, or when life wasn't working out for me – pull out the 'you owe me' card, remind her of 'all I've given up' for her to be in Oxford. Secondly, while I was floundering, I always knew Merryn was praying for me. She was with me in the difficulty, ready to talk through possibilities and silly ideas.

Championing one another today

Merryn's a medical statistician, I'm a writer and speaker. I work with words; she works with numbers. We come from different worlds! Because our professional lives are so different, we don't have much opportunity to promote each other's work or open doors of opportunity for each other. Instead, we champion each other privately. Wins are celebrated. When I get a new book contract or she wins a new research grant, we're straight off to the restaurant to celebrate. And we try and create space for each other during life's stressful moments.

During the final months of writing my last book, I was significantly burned out for a variety of reasons. Merryn arranged weekend trips to help me recharge – just me, her, a picnic and our dog Rupert – and that proved pivotal to my getting through. Like most people, Merryn at times faces difficult situations at work requiring diplomacy, and many an afternoon has been spent talking and praying about ways forward. I think both of our professional lives would be the lesser without the other's presence. But it happens quietly, in the background, an unseen foundation that helps the building stand strong.

If you would like to read more of their story, Sheridan's book Resurrection Year *tells it in much more detail. Visit https:// sheridanvoysey.com to find out more about that and his other (beautifully written and incredibly helpful) books.*

Allowing others to champion you both

As married couples, we are not meant to be self-sufficient. God calls us to be a part of the body of Christ and that isn't just about being his representatives here on earth, his hands and feet as it were. It's because, as Ecclesiastes 4:9–10 beautifully illustrates:

> Two are better than one,
>   because they have a good return for their labour:
> if either of them falls down,
>   one can help the other up.

While this image is of two people, when we put it alongside the image of us as Christ's body in 1 Corinthians 12:21–27, we can see that God calls us to mutual support:

> The eye cannot say to the hand, 'I don't need you!' And the head cannot say to the feet, 'I don't need you!' . . . God has put the body together, giving greater honour to the parts that lacked it, so that there should be no division in the body, but that its parts should have equal concern for each other. If one part suffers, every part suffers with it; if one part is honoured, every part rejoices with it.

> Now you are the body of Christ, and each one of you is a part
> of it.

We can be encouraging and spurring one another on, as individuals but also as couples, when we have people that we trust around us. We can listen to God's Word for their lives and be open when they do the same for us. As our friendships deepen, and we know we are all totally for one another, we can share openly about our struggles (obviously if you are sharing things about your marriage without your partner in the room you need to ensure they are happy for you to do so). There are moments in which we can all celebrate with one another – but also those times when we feel life has given us a battering and we need our friends to help hold us up, to pray earnestly, speak truth courageously and reach out to us gently.

In the day-to-day too, it is so helpful to have those outside of your marriage to bring you encouragement and champion your cause. Even with the best of intentions, we can get quite inward looking as couples when our daily routines are so busy. Taking time out with trusted friends to pray and discuss what is going on really helps to lift our focus and renew our perspective; to see the bigger picture once again. The couple who think they don't need anyone else are in real danger of allowing that isolation to peck away at their relationship. If you don't have anyone you both feel comfortable sharing with, then we encourage you to start praying God either brings new people into your lives or shows you those already there that you could have this type of supportive relationship with.

> The couple who think they don't need anyone else are in real danger of allowing that isolation to peck away at their relationship.

Over to you

- In what ways do you consciously honour the other person over yourself? If you know this is something you need to work on, what steps can you take to cultivate this principle?
- If you recognize that your partner has taken the time to champion and honour you over and above themselves recently, do take the time to celebrate that and thank them.
- So often marriage books focus on love, but not too many mention cherishing. How did you respond to what you read about cherishing? Do you feel you are both good at cherishing each other, or are there ways you can be more intentional about doing this?

Grace for the Unexpected

In this world you will have trouble. But take heart! I have overcome the world.

John 16:33

Claire: You will have picked up through earlier chapters that our marriage has been full of the unexpected. I had no idea I would struggle so much to cope with Steve's hours as a record producer, we didn't expect to almost become yet another statistic when I decided I could no longer cope with our marriage. And I certainly didn't expect to become a pastor's wife! We didn't expect to lose Steve's dad two weeks after our first child was born. Or for us to watch my sister go through two divorces, the second one particularly difficult as it devastated her family too. And, while my mum had been ill for most of my life, we didn't expect her to suffer as she did for so long, before she finally went to be with Jesus while we were writing this book.

That might all sound quite dramatic, and yet our lives aren't that different from other people's. Somehow, in our Western culture, suffering doesn't seem to be expected – and so it seems that much harder to deal with when it inevitably comes. The truth is, every couple reading this book will face unexpected trials and difficulties. There will be events that gatecrash your lives and you are left reeling – whether it directly affects both of you or one in particular.

How we respond to these difficulties really will shape us as people. Because our culture teaches us to seek happiness and comfort, we can often protest against the unexpected, asking God why it is happening to us and begging him to take it away. And yet, if we stop and think about who our heavenly Father is, he is the God of all eternity – of space and time. God knows exactly what is going to happen to us, so none of the things that threaten to derail us take him by surprise. And, as we looked at in Chapter 10, if Jesus told his disciples to expect trouble, but still to take heart in him, why are we surprised when difficulties come?

> God knows exactly what is going to happen to us, so none of the things that threaten to derail us take him by surprise.

I read Jerry Sittser's book *A Grace Disguised*[1] soon after my mum died, at the recommendation of many people. I can see why. The tag line for the book is 'How the soul grows through loss' and he really tackles the deep questions and utter anguish we can have after an unexpected loss (his wife, mum and daughter were killed in a head-on collision). I was fascinated by what he said in his chapter 'The Terror of Randomness'. He would spend time imagining what would have happened if they hadn't been on the road at the particular moment the other car came careering down the opposite side, out of control. If he'd just asked his kids to go to the toilet before embarking on the journey beforehand, for instance. Then his brother-in-law challenged him, saying that he would never want that power – did he really want to know about what unexpected events might occur in the future so that he could avoid them? But then he'd need to know what other accidents might happen as a result of that changed path. He realized that he needed to stop trying to control what happened in life.

It is that issue of control that is so key. We are taught by society that we are the masters of our own destiny, and that we should do all we can to grab hold of all we desire. And yet one of the biggest lessons the global Covid-19 pandemic taught us is that, however secure we try and make our future and however in control we feel, none of us knows what tomorrow will bring. Uncertainty breeds anxiety as plans go out the window. Yet that anxiety led many to question the meaning of life and what they were living for in the first place. If we look to the Bible, Jesus' teaching is super clear – but probably very different to what we have been conditioned to expect:

> Anyone who intends to come with me has to let me lead. You're not in the driver's seat, *I* am. Don't run from suffering; embrace it. Follow me and I'll show you how. Self-help is no help at all. Self-sacrifice is the way, my way, to finding yourself, your true self. What kind of deal is it to get everything you want but lose yourself? What could you ever trade your soul for?
>
> Matthew 16:24–26, *The Message*

Jesus says quite plainly that we need to let him lead and, when we do, he may well take us into the way of suffering. Actually, perhaps we need to take more heed of his words; it may mean that the suffering we experience in this life won't seem so unexpected.

As we looked at in the chapter on taking responsibility for ourselves (Chapter 8), the way we respond to suffering really does impact our maturity as Christians which, in turn, affects our marriages. How many of us can truly say that we welcome suffering in the way that Paul describes here?

> We boast in the hope of the glory of God. Not only so, but we also glory in our sufferings, because we know that suffering produces perseverance; perseverance, character; and character, hope. And hope does not put us to shame, because God's love has been poured out into our hearts through the Holy Spirit, who has been given to us.
>
> Romans 5:2–5

Finding the light for today

Patrick and Diane Regan are the energetic, passionate founders of the incredible charity Kintsugi Hope,[2] which seeks to open up honest conversations in churches today. It wasn't that long ago that both were busy in different jobs, but a period of unexpected challenges caused them to make some big changes to their lives. We interviewed them about how they navigated what seemed like a relentless onslaught together as a couple.

Patrick: We went through one of those seasons in our lives where everything went wrong at once. It started with our daughter Keziah getting a condition called HSP (Henoch–Schönlein purpura), which is a condition where you get spots (purpura) across your body, mainly on your legs; it lasts six to eight weeks and can also give you temporary arthritis. It also means if you have a temperature or you feel sick you need to be rushed into hospital as it can affect your kidneys – she had that three times in three years. And then my dad got cancer followed by Diane's dad, who also got cancer.

We went to Center Parcs for a break – we got a break, but not quite what we were expecting, as Daniel [our son] broke his leg. Then Abi [our daughter] at ten weeks old got diagnosed with nystagmus, a visual impairment. And I got diagnosed with a degenerative knee condition, which meant I needed to get both my legs broken in three places, an external frame put around each leg with pins being drilled into my bones and the wires going through one side and out the other side. I was told I would need it on both legs, at different times. The external frame would be on for between six to eighteen months each time. There's quite a big risk of infection, so Diane would have to clean the frame every day.

Diane: When our dads had cancer, I had an unexpected pregnancy. We were just getting our heads around it, even though I always wanted number four. We got excited, and even told the kids; I guess by the time you get to number four you are more relaxed about it all. So when it came to me spotting, I'd spotted the previous time so I thought: 'Oh great it's just an early opportunity to go and see baby, like last time.' I did not even imagine that there would be anything wrong and so I went to that appointment on my own. I texted Patrick simply saying: 'Sorry babe.' I didn't want to talk about it and I had to have surgery.

Patrick: The challenge after that was Diane still wanting us to try for another child. She really wanted to and I didn't, so we had to work through that process. The legs were making it worse because time was ticking: we knew that once I actually had the leg op, then there was no chance that Diane would be able to look after a baby and look after me. So we decided to go for another child before the first operation. But Diane went into labour and it all went wrong. She had to have an emergency caesarean, she lost 2.8 litres of blood and I thought she was going to die; she turned completely yellow. Caleb was born, but the whole experience was really traumatic.

Diane and I met when I was 15, so we've been together our whole lives and it was so frightening to see her like that. I'm a bit of a fixer, and when I can't fix something, I have to live with this sense of really wanting to try to fix it – actually all I could do was love and care, be there and pray and live with the mystery. I'm typically the glass is half empty type of person and with Diane the glass is always half full.

Emotional challenges

Diane: I think Patrick's own journey with mental health started right back when he was first diagnosed with his leg condition. We didn't even know what depression or anxiety was then. Around that time he was given a sabbatical. On the outside people thought: 'Oh, isn't that wonderful? They've got three months together, just the two of them.' The kids were at school, and I was pregnant with Abi at the time. Actually, it was one of the hardest, loneliest times ever because it meant Patrick stopped, and everything caught up with him. I spent every day picking him up off the floor, and no one had any idea. He was struggling with pain in his body, without even knowing what it was. And he was processing so much from years and years and years of carrying on regardless. It was a very long journey of understanding and accepting that this is life. I'm very much an optimist and quite strong (not so strong now), but again it was learning I couldn't fix him. I didn't have the tools and the skills; I wished I was a doctor. Health was one of his biggest anxieties. So I'd be always googling and looking up things, but I'd have to admit I didn't know the answer.

Patrick: The hardest thing with that is you struggle with health anxiety, and then you go to the doctor and everyone's going, 'Oh it's just going to be a little knee problem,' and it became a keyhole surgery that was a hundred times worse – even worse than I had imagined it to be.

When I started that sabbatical, I knew things were really difficult and that it was affecting all of us. When I turned up at an appointment with a counsellor and described this whole catalogue of events, she replied: 'What do you expect?' For us, the whole anxiety/depression was about trying to be strong for too long. It was the combination of the physical challenges of life, along with the mental and emotional challenges.

I was also very conscious of the effect it all had on Diane. She wrote a chapter in *When Faith Gets Shaken*[3] about second-hand smoke. The whole idea is that second-hand smoke can still kill you. This was true particularly when the leg issue was going on, and Diane's mental health started to be affected so she went on medication.

Diane: I felt very alone actually, because Patrick was so busy preparing for being off for six months that he detached himself from what was going to happen. I don't know how he did it, because even on the day of the surgery he walked in so cool and calm. At this point, I was trying to hold it all together, as I knew I had to be strong. I knew he was going to crash, and I knew I had to be there. So I went on medication to help myself just get through that.

All the attention is on the person going through the difficulty, and yet there's much research done that states that by the time you reach the age of 46, 50 per cent of people will have been in a caring situation, which shocked me. It's very hard work, it's lonely and there's limited support and recognition actually out there. When you're caring for someone, often you don't then look after yourself.

I was worried that I would feel resentful and so, particularly before the operation, I spent time looking up how to change my role from being a wife to being a carer. And all I found were depressing forums for people caring for loved ones, typically with dementia or mental health issues. And the carers were all becoming very resentful and very bitter, which was exactly what I was afraid of.

Grace for each day

Patrick: There were moments when we felt anger, and then guilty about being angry – but then we realized that the psalms are full of lament. Anger is actually an emotional response to pain. It's not anger that's the issue, because often there's a sense of injustice, and actually what we were going through was pretty unfair. I felt like saying to God: 'I've worked really hard my whole life and given everything to you, you know. Why is this going on? I just don't get it!' And so needing to process that was an issue. We learned loads about what self-compassion was and what self-compassion wasn't. I used to think self-compassion was a bubble bath and candles. And that sounded boring to me. It sounded good to Diane but I'm not into that at all.

Then I realized that actually self-compassion takes so much discipline. It is really about talking to yourself the way that you talk to your best friend. We learned to get curious about what each other was thinking about. Diane used to say to me: 'Your mind is not your friend'; not every thought you have is a fact and so don't believe everything you think. That's what we constantly say to each other still, and today I talk a lot about doubt and how it is actually a really useful thing. Questioning is actually quite healthy.

Diane: With the first leg operation, when Patrick came home by ambulance he was delivered by stretcher into the lounge and then the medical staff just left, and the enormity of what I was having to do struck me. He couldn't move, was in absolute agony, spaced out and a box of drugs was given to me – the kids were all around too. I ended up running away upstairs as I felt the tunnel was just too long and I could not see the light at the end of it. I remember just saying: 'God, I cannot do this.' The enormity of it hit me. And God just gently said: 'Don't look for light at the end of the tunnel, look for it here and now. Just get enough for now.'

That became our strategy for coping: just getting enough for today. Sometimes it was just getting enough for the next five minutes – whatever length of time we felt we could cope with. Sometimes it was about simply knowing that there was still so much good around. Because there *was* kindness: neighbours were doing kind things, there were little breakthroughs, and so we learned to look really hard to find them. Knowing that God was there in it and was sending enough for us to be able to get through that little bit was what got us through the first operation.

I had to make adjustments to his frame, knowing I was inflicting pain. I viewed it as a job that had to be done to get through to the other side, so I knew there was a reason why it was happening. Afterwards, reflecting on it, it was quite overwhelming. In the beginning I was shaking, but you quickly just get into it. You have to readjust, and then at each entry point, because it's going into the bone, into the leg, into the tissue, you have to clean the pins and struts and you have to be in a completely sterile environment. I'm not a nurse, never wanted to be a nurse, still don't want to be a nurse, but I became an expert in keeping things sterile, even with four kids and a dog.

I think I did become a bit resentful at times; I think I did get quite angry, because I'd be so exhausted and then Patrick would ask me to do something. But it wasn't his fault so I would then feel guilty about feeling like that.

Here we go again . . .

And then the second operation loomed. By this time, we'd actually moved out of London and it almost felt like it was all too big a challenge for us to cope with. Although we were closer to our family it was almost alien – like we were in a new land almost. I felt like we were a tiny boat being tossed around an ocean with no idea where we were going to land. We had just found some lyrics from a song by Iona 'Beyond These Shores'. The words talk about how we don't know where we're going to arrive or even if we are going to arrive. But God has gone before us and if we sink to the depths of below he is there. That was what I held on to, even though we felt like we were this little tiny boat.

I couldn't comprehend, I couldn't come up with the answers, I couldn't come up with solutions. I had no idea how it was going to end and I just had to give it to God, and so my conclusion became that life's tough but so much tougher without God. My faith has been simplified to that as a result of all we went through.

Patrick: I think all of the pressure did affect the relationship. We could have got really, really resentful and didn't, and we didn't get really angry at each other as we could have done, but it was affected.

Diane: Yes, I think we learned to recognize that sometimes you each need to vent and allow the other to do so. And also work out the times when you do need to try and respond. But it's so important to have that honesty and have that outlet. And also, to understand that sometimes it's all going to bubble over, but it doesn't mean that I'm attacking you personally. So we had to learn to give each other the space to do this.

Patrick: That's where I think the resilience stuff comes in. You learn how to adapt and be flexible, and lower your standards. Lots of people visited and Diane hates it if the house is a tip, but we had to learn that people would understand.

With the first operation, I had a major panic attack at the hospital, which was scary. But the second time around, psychologically it was harder because we knew what was coming. Diane couldn't even talk about it. It was a really difficult experience doing it again, knowing what to expect.

Lasting change

We've always said we'd never want to go through it again. But still, we recognize the incredible change it's made in us. For example, I think we're less judgmental. I always felt that we were hot on values, but actually, success for us now is much more about following our heart, doing what we believe God's called us to do, and being ourselves rather than conforming to be something we are not. Without such times, which forced those issues, our charity Kintsugi Hope wouldn't exist.

For other couples going through unexpected difficulty, I would just like to say that courage and vulnerability are intertwined, and not to be scared of vulnerability. It's hard to think of something courageous that doesn't involve vulnerability. I think that typically blokes do not understand that – we can say it, but we don't understand it.

Also, I think there were times when Diane probably wanted me to respond in a certain way, and I just couldn't. And I think there were other moments when I wanted her to respond in a certain way, and she didn't. In those moments you can't control, you can't manipulate, you can't fix. Sometimes you just have to be there. And that's the hardest thing; I think that was definitely a massive learning curve.

Diane: Yes, and acknowledging that when you're just so exhausted, it's hard to be that loving person. But trusting and knowing each other well enough to know that just because your partner is having a bad day doesn't mean that they don't love you. We can't just get our support from the other person, as it's really difficult for them as well. So I would say, learn not to rely on the other person for everything. For me, I'd be so empty I had to go back to God to get the love and to get energy.

The making or breaking of us

We know that many of the hard things we face in life are used by God to make us more like Jesus. The why and how behind all of that may remain a mystery to us for the rest of our lives, but that is what we see biblical characters such as Job, Joseph, Paul and Peter learned. However, sometimes the unexpected can really cause us to feel off-kilter. If we are both facing a really difficult situation, how can we face it together rather than taking out our pain and frustration on one another? And if one of us has to face the unexpected, how can the other support them well?

When a seemingly random disaster occurs, it can often be the making or breaking of a relationship. During the 2020 lockdown, some couples certainly found their marriages were under extra pressure. Tragically, statistics showed an increase in domestic abuse and violence during this time. However, as Harry Benson, a researcher from Marriage Foundation, discovered, there was also an increase in relationships being strengthened: 'In our research, we found that twice as many marriages improved during lockdown compared to those that worsened. Although stress levels did indeed rise, many people found a fresh resolve to invest in their relationships and prioritise them more.'[4]

When the whole world around us seems to be turning upside down we appear to have a choice: we can turn to one another, even cling to each other, tending gently to our partner. Alternatively, we can take our frustration and pain out on them as they are the person closest to us. We have experienced, and initiated, both responses and the former is definitely the preferable and most edifying one! As we mentioned in 'Championing one another in the hardest of times' in Chapter 10, a recent blow to us as a family had us learning afresh how to trust God and come to him together, supporting the other when they were struggling to deal with the situation and being open about our own struggles too.

Of course, when something unexpected happens it can change things forever, or at least for a sustained period of time. It may be that as a couple we have to get used to a new 'normal', which may involve praying, discussing and renegotiating the way that life happens and our roles within that.

Whenever difficulties occur, prayer (both individually but also, very importantly, together) is a vital response. When we pray, we commit our circumstances to God and invite his wisdom into our decision-making. Sadly, when we are thrown by the unexpected, we may feel like prayer is the last thing we want to do. Too often we can hide from God, or stop talking to him – but when we push through in order to reconnect, we are reaching out to the very source of life itself, and to the one who *does* understand what we are going through.

It may be that we find ourselves in situations that make us question God's very nature. When that happens, it is really important to give one another the chance to vocalize how they are feeling – without judgement (see Sheridan's story in Chapter 10). Emotions are God-given: whether we feel despair, anger, frustration or deep questioning it is OK to say so. He already knows what we are thinking and feeling – often our vocalizing is simply helping us to process, and giving our partner the opportunity to understand and be involved in that.

Learning to lament

Claire: It is at this point that I think the psalmists can really teach us something invaluable; I have certainly found myself turning to the psalms when faced with something unexpected that seems overwhelming – or when ministering to others (including my husband) who are facing hard times.

For example, I have used the Psalms to help me express the pain of beginning to lose my mum (as it was such a long process), of not understanding why a young mum in our church died, of feeling helpless to change the situation my sister and nieces faced, and of finally being confronted with death head on as I spent the last moments of mum's journey here on earth with her. I've also turned to them in the moments when I've felt lonely in our marriage, or when I know I've messed up and caused problems in our relationship.

It was actually when I found myself living back with my parents after I had left Steve and then the other guy had left me that I first realized that there were psalms that vocalized exactly how I felt. These were the words that I recorded in my journal at that time: 'My wounds fester and are loathsome because of my sinful folly. I am bowed down and brought very low; all day long I go about mourning . . . I am feeble and utterly crushed; I groan in anguish of heart' (Psalm 38:5–6,8).

When I began grieving, I remembered how deeply I had connected with the Psalms then, and so I turned back to them. It was at that point that I realized how many are actually laments. The lament psalms give us permission to express our confusion, hurt, weariness and questions about why life isn't as we expected it to be. As Christians, we can be ashamed of feeling confused, which means we may look down on our partner if they are struggling. And yet God has provided us with a means of expressing those deep, dark emotions that we *do* all experience at some point in our lives. God isn't fazed by them, and so we need to learn not to be (whether it is us or our partner experiencing them).

The truth is, we are all broken and are all in the process of being made more like Jesus. Rather than hiding our grief and confusion, we need to give one another the space to vocalize how we are feeling. And actually, being as open and honest as the psalmists takes real courage and faith; to say to God we don't understand, that we don't feel he is there and yet to still choose to affirm our trust in him is a massive step of faith. So many of the psalmists end their writing by remembering God's faithfulness; they anchor themselves to what they know about God. In Psalm 77, for example, the writer talks about God redeeming his people through the exodus (see vv.10–20). For us today, our ultimate deliverance is found in the cross.

> Rather than hiding our grief and confusion, we need to give one another the space to vocalize how we are feeling.

The Bible even includes psalms that simply reflect the writers' grief and anguish without offering up any tidy solutions (such as Psalm 88). We seem to find that difficult, because we want and expect resolution. But that is reflective of life, and often our journey includes learning to give up our right to understand everything that happens. And if our partner is currently on a journey of learning that, we need to be supportive rather than trying to rush to fix or resolve how they are feeling.

Accepting help

It is important to recognize that there are times in our lives when we need extra support from outside the marriage – and that's OK. As we have seen, that is why we are part of a community. We had experience of this again recently when I was staying at my parents' to help with mum's care as she was dying. I was away much longer than any of us were expecting; our church rallied around and helped Steve practically by providing meals for him and the kids (and then all of us once I was home). We also received cards with loving messages and, once home, I had gifts and flowers given to me. But, most of all, I remember the night before my mum died. Steve and the kids had considered coming down to visit (as it was a Saturday), but the kids had a lot on and we were all tired, so they thought it might be wiser to stay at home. My two closest friends from church spoke to one another and decided they would drive down simply to show me support. There were some messages back and forth. Having spoken to Steve I felt mum was close to the end and he and the kids should come again simply to say a proper goodbye, so my friends thought

> There are times in our lives when we need extra support from outside the marriage – and that's OK.

perhaps they wouldn't come. But in the end they all came. In all honesty, I was quite apprehensive; it had been just our family for quite a few days, and life felt like a really surreal 'bubble' at that point. I also didn't think I could cope with other people's grief.

The day before, a close friend of my sister had popped by with a meal for us, and it was actually enough to feed us all on the Saturday. During their visit, one of my friends took some time to be with Mum and started singing over her as she felt led; gradually, one by one, we joined her and had a beautiful time singing worship songs around Mum's bedside, which had actually been her wish for her death. We were all so wrung out by that point that I'm not sure that would have happened if my friend hadn't instigated it, and I look back on that time now so grateful that it took place.

More generally, Steve and I have been blessed over the years to have small groups of friends that we have been able to share with and who have supported us through whatever has happened in our lives. Even though we hadn't fully explained the extent to which our marriage was broken, we still had a group of three other couples who quickly came together to pray for our marriage when I left Steve. Since we have been in church leadership, we've known the support of a small group of people who came together specifically to pray for us regularly. And we have a few couples that we know we can say anything to and they will still be there, supporting, praying, encouraging and challenging us. We've also sought mentors in order to have them speak wisdom into our lives. This life can be full of joy, but it is also difficult to navigate at times. Having such outside support is so helpful when we face the inevitable yet unexpected pain in life.

Over to you

- Do you expect to experience suffering in your marriage? Why or why not? Discuss your thoughts on suffering together, and what your individual responses to it are – and then consider whether you are drawn closer or further apart through suffering. If you feel that you are being pushed apart, take some time to prayerfully discuss what steps you can put in place to stay connected. Together, ask God to work in your situation and help you draw closer to one another.

- What do you think of the idea of vulnerability being truly courageous? Are you ever vulnerable enough to allow others to help you in difficult times?

- Have you ever engaged with lament as an individual? As a couple? Perhaps, at an appropriate time, you could find a psalm that expresses the difficult emotions you are feeling and share that with your partner. Or you could write your own lament – separately or together.

12

Grace Lasts the Distance

Love bears all things, believes all things, hopes all things, endures all things.

1 Corinthians 13:7, ESV

Claire: As I look at the wedding photos we have up in our bedroom, I have a mix of feelings – nostalgia but also concern and sadness for my younger self. Little did I know what I was embarking on when I said my vows and started married life with Steve. I had no idea of the huge ups and downs we would face, and that there would be a time when I felt there could be no future for our marriage.

I am also reminded of what my university English tutor said when I told him I was getting married during the summer between my second and final years: 'You will look back one day and think what a quaint thing it was I did.' Wow that made me mad at the time – and it still makes me mad. How dare he be so patronizing! Yes, I was naive – totally naive – and yes, the statistics show that many marriages do not make it. And yes, we were getting married at an extremely young age. However, he was an embittered divorcee with an overly negative viewpoint of marriage. Here we stand today having weathered many storms but also having celebrated numerous high points. While we can frustrate each other deeply at times, we are also immensely grateful that we have one another to journey through life with. Knowing that there is another who knows me better than anyone else and who, when the rubber hits the road, is totally there for me, is a gift I know I can take for granted far too often. Yes, marriage is tough. It stretches us beyond what we think we can bear at times. But marriage is also beautiful.

We have been married for nearly thirty years now, so feel we have some idea of what has helped us to navigate that time. Sometimes it has been a case of just clinging on – dogged determination not to become another statistic, as Steve shared earlier. But before we share more from our own story, let's hear from Wendy Virgo, who has been married to Terry for more than half a century:

Grace has been the glue

Terry is known around the world for his preaching on grace; here Wendy reveals that grace has also been a hallmark of their more than fifty-year marriage.

Fifty-two years ago, I walked down a church aisle on my father's arm to join my fiancé, Terry, and make vows before God and the listening congregation. I promised to love, honour and obey him, and I meant it. After all, how hard could it be? We were in love! We loved God, we loved each other, and we wanted to conduct our lives in a way that was honouring to him. We wanted to obey what the Bible said about Christian marriage, and so if it said that a wife should honour and obey her husband, I was prepared to do that: until, of course, about two weeks in when Terry wanted to do something that I disagreed with! I soon found out that believing in a principle is one thing, but carrying it out in actual life is another. So, did I abandon my vows? Adjust my thinking? Assume that only the naive and simple could stick to such promises?

Little did we know that we were at the beginning of a fifty-year-plus-journey, and that we would still be working out the vows we made to each other that day. Saying those vows out loud was very important to me. I was stating before God and witnesses that I took God's Word seriously, and remembering that has often made me pause and bite my tongue before I exploded into saying or doing something that could have had damaging repercussions.

Terry and I are very different in temperament. He is even-tempered, more easy going and placid than me, strong and consistent. I tend to be more intense, quick to give opinions, less patient. But doesn't God often bring people together who are vastly different? We have often remarked on that and seen how couples grow and mature as they learn to appreciate each other's strengths, forgive their weaknesses and adapt as they grow their marriage.

The transforming lessons of grace

Soon after our wedding, we went to live in the small town where Terry had recently become the pastor of a new church, so, when we returned from our honeymoon, we were virtually church planting, with very little idea of what that meant. In 1968, we knew of no one else who was taking this route. We just knew that we had to follow the Bible and listen to the Holy Spirit as far as we could understand. So, while we were building a marriage and a home, we were also building a church.

Like any young couple, there were highs and lows, struggles and misunderstandings, but also a lot of joy and laughter. I was only 22, so I had a lot of growing up to do and sometimes shudder to think how I blundered around trying to learn, not only how to be a wife, but how to relate to the people in our congregation!

Meanwhile, Terry was on a very significant journey of discovery. It was several years before he began to grasp, preach and apply the wonderful truth of the grace of God. In those days, churches and individual Christians often laboured under a sense of guilt and condemnation that robbed us of joy and the awareness of God's unconditional love. But as Terry took us through the book of Romans, unfolding the amazing revelation that 'Therefore, there is now no condemnation for those who are in Christ Jesus, because through Christ Jesus the law of the Spirit who gives life has set you free from the law of sin and death', a transformation began. As we all began to grasp it, we learned not to live in guilt for our faults and failures but to enjoy the goodness of God and receive his forgiveness and to forgive and love each other.

This, of course, was huge for every aspect of life and, as I look back now, I see how it affected our marriage. Living in the freedom of God's grace means that we learn to give grace to others. It does not mean that we condone wrongs and sin, but it does mean that we try to handle them with empathy, humility and understanding. A key verse for me at one time was Ephesians 4:32: 'Be kind and compassionate to one another, forgiving each other, just as in Christ God forgave you.' God in his great mercy has forgiven me. Therefore, I have a reservoir of forgiveness to draw on to forgive others, and that sometimes includes my husband and vice versa!

The importance of prayer . . . and rest

Terry is known for his preaching and writing on the grace of God, but he is also a man of prayer. This has been immensely important in our marriage. At times, especially when the children were small and life was particularly hectic, we were not able to pray together every day, but we made sure that we prayed as frequently as possible. Now that they are all grown up, we pray together most days. This is a huge factor in keeping us close and open with one another, for as you pray you hear each other's heart and share visions, hopes and longings.

Another important factor in our marriage is that we have always guarded a day off. For us, this has been a Monday. However busy we have been (and with five children, church leading and planting, hospitality, travel and all the rest of the minutiae of a church leader's life, believe me, it has been busy!) I have had the joy of knowing that on Mondays I have Terry's full attention, and he has time to relax. We don't do anything very groundbreaking: walk, talk, have lunch in a pub, maybe go to the cinema – basically unwind. I believe that this also is a spin-off from living in the grace of God. He is not a hard taskmaster; we don't have to keep doggedly working ourselves into the ground to earn his approval; we can enjoy his goodness to us in rest and recreation.

The power of marriage

Terry and I had faith for our marriage because we believed God had called us together; but faith is worked out. It has to be applied. It means: 'If God called us to this, then we have the capacity to do this'; 'If God brought us together, we can work together despite our differences'; 'If God called us together, we can keep loving each other'; 'If God brought us together, we can say "no" to temptations, and "yes" to unexpected challenges'.

And those vows to honour and obey? Basically, we have found that love includes mutual respect. When decisions have had to be made, we have discussed the issues and come to an agreement. Sometimes – not often – it has been hard to come to an agreement, and that is when Terry makes the final call. That requires faith and grace on my part, but I have learned that I can trust him, as a man who prays and walks humbly with God. So 'obeying' has not been a big issue, but it has been an underlying attitude.

A strong Christian marriage is powerful. When a high-profile marriage breaks up the fall-out is disastrous. We have an enemy who hates marriage and is constantly undermining it, seeking to belittle it and trivialize it because it has the potential to say something profound about the nature and character of God. I am so grateful for the grace of God, which has kept us deeply loving each other, appreciating each other – and having fun together after all these years. What a gift!

Standing firm

Claire: It can sound so simple to say we will stick to our marriage vows come what may, and yet that flies in the face of what our culture constantly drip feeds us. Relationships are often viewed as transient and disposable, so it is now counter-cultural to live a faithful, married life. I was fascinated to read what blogger, author and friend Lucy Rycroft wrote on her blog about the lessons she has learned about marriage from the Netflix series *The Crown*.[1] Obviously a work of fiction, she spoke of how refreshing it was 'that the script has been written to highlight tensions and situations that are very believable . . . One thing I particularly like is the way Queen Elizabeth and Prince Philip's marriage is portrayed, warts and all.'

Despite the fact they are not a 'normal' couple, the Queen and Prince Philip undoubtedly face the same struggles that other couples do. There must be times when one of them finds the other tiresome, or they simply feel like they are out of touch with one another. In her blog, Lucy looks at an episode during which the Queen finishes a gruelling world tour, Philip goes on his own tour for a month, and when he comes back there is a scene depicting the Queen speaking candidly about the fact that they are not able to opt for divorce. She asks Prince Philip what it would take for him to be wholeheartedly committed to their marriage again.

While we understand there are circumstances in which divorce may be the right option (infidelity or abuse for example), I do wonder whether we still hold to the view that divorce is 'not an option' for us. So many of the messages we hear in our culture are about what is best for us personally: if our marriage is no longer convenient, our partner no longer attentive – let's do what will make us happy, even if that means destroying our marriage. But that is not the way of the cross. Self-sacrifice and asking the hard questions are key to lasting the distance.

One of the ways we can ensure longevity in our marriages is by refusing to be swayed by our culture, which is so focused on self-gratification. It is so important that we ask ourselves, and our partners, regularly how committed we are to our marriages. We need to be honest in our answers too. It may be that distance has crept in without us really realizing it. It is so easy for that to happen: we can both be so busy, focused on our own 'to do' lists and simply getting through each day that we forget to include our partners in our daily lives.

Busyness is often one of the tactics that the devil likes to use, as it is so easy for us all to get caught up in it. It is vital to remember that we are in a battle and, as Ephesians 6 says, we need to be able to stand firm in it: 'put on the full armour of God, so that when the day of evil comes, you may be able to stand your ground, and after you have done everything, to stand' (v.13).

I have heard the phrase, 'The couple that prays together, stays together,' many times over the years. This might sound like a corny soundbite, but there is so much truth in it. Praying for and with one another is a really helpful and healthy way of ensuring we stay on the same page. It is difficult to pray together when we are arguing, so it can force the issue of needing to sort out any differences. But it also shows that we are in our relationship for the long haul, as we usually pray about those things we care most about.

Recognizing that marriage has seasons

Steve: There are times when marriage seems like the sweetest gift straight from heaven – and others when it is simply hard graft that we would rather not do. It's important that we are honest about that, rather than trying to pretend otherwise. We can remember speaking to a couple about handling conflict: they were adamant that they never argued – and never would. As people who are usually vocal about issues we disagree on, we found it quite hard to believe them. But, give them their due, their marriage did seem to be very harmonious. A few years later, Claire did have a conversation with the wife in which she admitted that she'd been totally thrown by the fact that they had argued. She was beginning to learn that, while our relationships may have grown through mutual love and respect, there will be times when we disagree. Learning to discuss issues we have differing opinions on without creating lasting conflict is really important. Often the quieter partner will keep quiet for fear of causing a scene, but we have seen too many times how that simply leads to silent discontent and bitterness. As we mention in Chapter 7, it is so important for both people to feel heard and understood in a constructive way.

We were once at a marriage weekend where we were encouraged to always argue holding a cushion while touching knees. We both found that hilarious and slightly preposterous. The point being made was that the person with the pillow was allowed to speak uninterrupted and the touching knees meant that you were still in gentle physical contact with your partner. While we may have laughed at that suggestion, it certainly did highlight the need to find a way to talk more constructively than we were doing. (And the truth is, it is hard to stay mad at each other when you end up having a cushion fight while trying to touch knees!)

We have already talked about a few of the different seasons we've been through in previous chapters, such as long hours at work causing loneliness and distance between us, the emotional rollercoaster of becoming parents, navigating the times when one of us has had particular developments in our career and the unpredictability of grief.

> Life doesn't stand still and so our marriages have to have a certain elasticity to them.

We have also weathered periods of ill health, difficulties within friendships, times of deep depression and myriad other seasons. The point is, life doesn't stand still and so our marriages have to have a certain elasticity to them. As couples, while we may have worked diligently on a vision statement early on in marriage, and been exceedingly clear about how we were going to make time for one another every day, there will be periods when our plans need to be revised – when we need to learn to be more flexible and creative. What once worked well may no longer be appropriate; we might need to learn to let go of good routines to find the best ones for the season we are in.

For example, having small children and then, as we are finding now, teenagers in the home, creates various challenges to spending quality time together; we have gone from being too tired after a day of working and looking after small children to stoke the romantic fires, to often going to sleep before our daughter does now!

Claire: You have heard how I allowed myself to get bitter about being left on my own so much as a young married woman, and how that caused me to look elsewhere for affirmation and love when I shouldn't have. When I first gave birth, Steve could have used that as an excuse to look at other women, as my body was tired and my emotions dark. But, like we all should as partners, he remained faithful and actually went out of his way to look for ways in which he could support me, rather than pointing out how I wasn't managing to keep up with the expectations we'd both set for our marriage. God calls each one of us to persevere in our faith – and that includes in our relationships with one another. When one of us (or even both of us) struggles, rather than turning our backs on the marriage, we need to recognize the season we are in, bring it to God in prayer and ask him to help us sustain the relationship – and help one another in it. Our prayers may be desperate, but they show we are looking for hope in the right place.

> Our prayers may be desperate, but they show we are looking for hope in the right place.

Keeping the main thing the main thing

The phrase, 'Keeping the main thing the main thing' was something I heard a conference speaker, whom I greatly admire, say in a talk. She was speaking about God at the time, but it struck me recently that this can be a helpful phrase for marriage too.

I don't know about you, but I have found the ongoing habits of my husband can really drain the joy out of our relationship. And I know he can say the same about me and my habits. Except it's not really our habits that cause the problems if we're being truly honest – it's how we respond to them.

Just to give you one example: I used to get exceedingly irritated when Steve rushed around trying to find his glasses and keys, even after the time he and our son should have left for the school run. More often than not, I'm sorry to say, I wasted even more time reminding him that he should have been more organized and got things ready the night before, as he knew he had the same routine each morning. Sadly, this meant we were often arguing just as our son was leaving for primary school, which did not set him up well (and was a bad way for me to say goodbye to him). As soon as the door shut and the car left our drive, I settled down with my cup of tea and Bible, and was usually totally overcome with gratitude that I got to take that time with God rather than having to be on the school run myself. I was exceedingly grateful that my husband was happy to do it. These days, I get up earlier to be with both our children before they travel to their secondary schools, as I'm a morning person. But when we were still taking our son to primary school, Steve drove him on most days, as he knows how much I hate driving.

That's just a small example – but it was a regular irritant that reared up a lot in our daily lives. It had the potential to ruin all of our days, by putting us in a bad mood before we had even really got started. Before I got to the point of opening my mouth and whinging at Steve for losing his keys yet again, I had a split-second choice: is this an issue that it is worth creating disharmony in our home over? Or can I simply choose not to speak, and instead help with the search for the keys? As my blogging friend, Tiffany Montgomery, wrote for a guest post on gratitude within marriage: 'Maybe he does always forget the trash in the morning. Is that the hill you want your marriage to die on?'[2]

Prioritizing each other

One of the simplest ways I try and show Steve that I am prioritizing him, is by not agreeing to social engagements with others without first checking with him. It might be frustrating for those around me at times, but usually I either say: 'Let me get back to you' or 'I think that should be alright, but I need to check with Steve first.' It may seem like overkill, but I do this with spending too. If I see something I would like to buy, I don't tend to buy it and then let him know; I view our money as a joint pot that we both have a say in, and so I usually just give him a quick ring to check he is happy for me to purchase the item. Hopefully that shows him that I am putting him rather than a material item first.

Steve: I know how much Claire appreciates me cooking. It is one of the things we loved doing together in the earlier years of our marriage when time allowed. So I prioritize time to cook and bake things that she doesn't normally prepare, to make it seem more special. Sometimes simply removing the strain of deciding what to cook can make a big difference and help your partner feel valued. I am currently learning that cleaning up the kitchen after you have cooked goes a long way too!

Continuing to romance

As working married people with children and with a church to lead, the list of responsibilities we carry can seem almost endless. All too often, we can find our catch-up times are simply focused on issues either with our children or with church members or situations. But it is necessary for us to make the time and space to do fun things. That requires actually planning these reconnection times into our diaries. But I think it also requires us to read the current situation and, where necessary, decide to break free from that plan to do something completely different. I know I am naturally more spontaneous than Claire (who prefers writing lots of lists and forward planning), but in particularly busy seasons of life, we have both found spontaneously doing something completely different has been so refreshing – whether that has meant 'pressing pause' to simply chill out together or deciding to go out and do a crazy fun thing.

> In particularly busy seasons of life, we have both found spontaneously doing something completely different has been so refreshing.

Lots of marriage preparation courses and marriage books talk about the need for setting aside a regular 'date night' that focuses simply on the two of you as a couple. Sadly, this is something that can often fall by the wayside after the first few years. It may be that you both have really busy jobs and are also heavily involved in church – having a night off together is a tall order these days! Or perhaps you are in the baby years of parenting, or have now passed into the teenage years when your kids are often up past your bedtime. At a recent leaders weekend away there was a talk on marriage, and one of the couples sharing said that the best piece of advice they had ever had was to get a lock fitted to the inside of their bedroom; this is something we are seriously considering doing for ourselves!

Intentional romancing

Judith and Jonathan Le Tocq are based in Guernsey, where Jonathan was formerly Chief Minister and is currently Minister for External Affairs. They are one of the couples whose wisdom we've enjoyed at various conferences over the years. Here they share how they learned the need for planning ahead when romancing one another, as well as some other helpful tips from a nearly 35-year-long marriage.

It was winter, Monday, and over breakfast we were informed via the local radio that as heavy snow began to fall, the Education Authority, faced with worsening conditions, had declared a 'snow day' and schools would be closed. Emily, 16, and a group of her friends decided to make use of the unique opportunity (it rarely snows in Guernsey) to visit the park, build snowmen and engage in snowball fights. Mid-morning, damp, rather exhausted and beginning to feel a little hungry, Emily phoned to see if anyone was at home and whether she could bring some friends back from the park. Her dad answered his mobile. Her friends waited to find out. The conversation was not long. 'We can't go to my place,' said Emily, putting her mobile back in her pocket. 'My mum and dad are having sex.'

In fact, we were at an appointment with a weight-loss counsellor. Not quite so romantic. But, when Emily phoned, we were in the middle of discussing important dietary details, and so once her dad had ascertained that there was no emergency he had simply responded: 'Not now, Emily, we're busy, you'll have to wait till we've finished.' Emily of course assumed that we were at home. She also knew that on our days off we often liked to make love in the middle of the day. Undisturbed. No kids around. No need to be so surreptitious or quiet.

As teenagers, our children had expressed a degree of disgust at discovering that their parents enjoyed creative lovemaking; indeed the concept of their parents having sex at all was apparently a decidedly unpleasant thought. Nevertheless, we regularly informed them that a) they wouldn't even be around to express such disgust if we'd never engaged in such activity, and b) the day would come when they would find themselves feeling grateful that their parents were still devoted to each other emotionally and physically, for the long term.

Being adaptable

Marriage goes through many changing seasons. We need to recognize these and adapt and respond accordingly. As newlyweds, especially before having children, finding time for romance and creative lovemaking was relatively easy. Despite being busy with jobs and engaged in church leadership, we didn't really have to plan such things; they seemed to occur regularly and naturally. During the baby and toddler season, we grew more tired, time was constrained, but we generally still had several evenings free. However, as the kids grew up, they got involved with more activities, which took up our time too. They also stayed up later – as teens they sometimes went to bed after us – they brought friends round, used our kitchen, seemed to make every room their own . . . you recognize the scene if you're in it! Romantic evenings at home when there seems to be a band rehearsing in one room, a re-enactment of *Bake Off* going on in the kitchen, athletics training in the garden, the whole place resembling and smelling like a youth hostel . . . are not that easy.

Here are a few tips that we have learned along the way, which have really helped us to continue to romance one another:

- We covenanted to hold each other to account and to regularly ask each other questions like, 'What three things do you like best about our life at the moment?' and, 'Where could I improve in serving and loving you?' or, 'What could we do practically to improve the quality of our time together?' Questions like these help keep us real with one another, thankful and constructive.
- We made mutual arrangements with peers who had kids of similar ages to us and who got on well with ours to undertake 'reciprocal sitting' when the kids were little so that, on a regular basis, we could get out for a romantic evening together. This developed into 'reciprocal holidays' on several occasions, where their kids came to stay with us while they had a few days away as a couple and vice versa. During certain busy seasons, this was a real blessing.
- We made space, sometimes at unusual times of the day (as mentioned above!) when we knew the kids would be out so that we could be intimate, make love and have fun together.

All this means being intentional and can take some serious planning. There's no real short cut for this, but we can testify that the fruits are well worth the effort.

Letting others in

We have looked at how as married couples we are not islands and therefore shouldn't try and do everything on our own. We have known couples who simply relied on one another, always closing ranks if anyone tried to ask how they were. This can,

> Being open to sharing our lives with those around us enables us all to be ministers of his grace.

ultimately, be quite isolating and also doesn't allow for the benefits of finding those we can share deeply with and give and receive support from. Ultimately, we are all part of God's family – our marriage is just one expression of that – and being open to sharing our lives with those around us enables us all to be ministers of his grace.

Judith and Jonathan Le Tocq were quite intentional right from early on in their marriage about finding a couple they could trust. They urge us all to:

> Get good advice and input from friends you trust and respect who are a few years down the track. We asked a couple who were around a decade ahead of us to 'speak into our lives' as we started out. They gave us permission to ask them questions and we gave them permission to challenge us to check we were working out our own solutions. This has proven invaluable.

Remembering well

Claire: I recently read in Gary Thomas' *Sacred Marriage* about the importance of remembering and telling each other the story of our marriage regularly. I felt a little smug: after all, the story of our marriage has become the subject of not just one but two books now! But then I felt challenged to think about whether I do take the time to remember, and also share with Steve, both the little and big moments of our marriage story. Of course, we have been through some incredibly difficult times and have seen God turn those around, restore and renew us and, amazingly, now use those very difficulties to fuel part of our ministry together. But there have been many other moments that have come and gone in our marriage and I wonder whether we take the time to either celebrate them, or remember soberly and thank God for his faithfulness through them.

I know I've written about the forgetfulness of Israel many times before (including in *Taking Off the Mask*). As they chose to fix their eyes on the problems directly in front of them, rather than remembering God delivering and sustaining them as a multitude of people, a distance crept into their relationship with him. We see again and again in the Old Testament how they turned to idols for fulfilment rather than God. If we forget about his faithfulness in bringing us this far, and forget that the ultimate goal of our marriage, and indeed our lives, is to make us more like Jesus to reflect him to the world around us, it is too easy for us to do the same in our marriages.

It is so important to take the time to stop and recognize all the good things that have happened in your marriage, as well as the difficult times God has brought you through.

Cultivating thankfulness

One of the biggest challenges God has given me in recent years is learning to be thankful. As I've already shared, I have a tendency towards negativity. Steve would back that up, and also say that one of the biggest challenges for him in our marriage has been my negativity.

It was back when I had postnatal depression that I first became aware that my struggles with mental health could cause me to find it exceedingly difficult to see beyond the place I felt trapped in. I had a toddler and a baby at the time, and attended an inter-church mums and toddlers group. Sometimes I simply went for the company, feeling quite numb about spiritual matters. But in one of the sessions, a friend of mine set us a gratitude challenge that impacted me hugely – and still does. Here she describes the effect it had on her personally:

> At the start of the New Year I gave out small notebooks to everyone, and asked them to write down five things each day that they are thankful for. It could be the same five things each day. Those who did it said it impacted them greatly. At the time, it helped me focus on the positives in my life. I was struggling with being a mum to a small child and feeling like I didn't have a life of my own. The biggest change came when I started to actively count all the good gifts in my life. It forced me to realize that God is good, very good, and we have been given so much. It honestly turned my life around and I had a fresh revelation of God's love for me through giving thanks.

When I tried it for myself, it lifted my spirit as well as my eyes – my whole perspective changed. It didn't take the difficulties away – I still wrestled with depression – but it helped me to see how God was still caring for me in the everyday and that I still had things that I could be grateful for. I can't say I do the gratitude challenge all the time, but when I notice that my attitude has worsened, when I'm feeling more negative generally, I try to begin my days by thanking God for five things – and often do the same when I go to bed at night.

This gratitude challenge can be helpful for all areas in our lives, including our marriages. As we've seen, all relationships go through different seasons and if you've been having a particularly difficult one, in which each day has felt like wading through thick mud, then taking time out to think about both the little and big things that you can be grateful to God for in your marriage is really beneficial. It provides a bigger perspective, helping you see beyond your current circumstances, and also reminds you of what God has been doing in your marriage – and, indeed, the gift that your marriage is to you.

Over to you

- How well do you celebrate and remember the big and small things that happen in your marriage?
- What season are you in within your marriage right now? Talk about what has changed, and any adjustments that you might need to make in order to thrive in this season.
- In what ways are you continuing to romance each other? If you've realized this is an area that has been neglected, decide together some ways you can kickstart the romance in your relationship again.

Epilogue

We began this book by acknowledging that marriage is hard work, but it is also a wonderful demonstration of the grace of God. Please remember that he is for you, and that he holds you both, whatever you face – individually and together – in this life. There may be moments of beauty that take your breath away and others that you feel you are hardly surviving. God's grace is sufficient for you both in every moment of every day.

We hope and pray that this book has been an encouragement, but also a challenge to you – to spur you on. If you would like to continue engaging with us, we will be regularly offering posts and blogs on marriage via Claire's website and Facebook page:

www.clairemusters.com
www.facebook.com/ClaireMustersWriter

Whether you felt you had a good marriage before you started reading, or picked up the book because you recognized you were struggling, remember and celebrate that God has a new portion of grace and mercy for you each day. As it says in Lamentations 3:22–23:

> Because of the LORD's great love we are not consumed,
>   for his compassions never fail.

They are new every morning;
>   great is your faithfulness.

God has everything you need to make your marriage a success:
a beautiful reflection of his love for his church. We will continue to pray for you – that you will grow deeper in your love
for him and for each other.

Acknowledgements

Creating a book is a long process, and there are many people behind the scenes who provide invaluable support. We just wanted to take the time to thank some of them here:

Thank you to the whole Authentic team – especially to Rachael Franklin and Donna Harris for believing in this book, as well as Charlotte Cuthbert for all her marketing help, editor Liz Williams and editorial administrator Becky Fawcett.

To all those who agreed to provide contributions for the book – you have added so much extra depth and we are so grateful for the wisdom shared, and the honesty with which you wrote.

We so appreciate those who agreed to read an early version of the manuscript and provide feedback, however large or small: thank you to Caz, Clare, Emma, Jed, Joe, Jonathan, Judith, Liz, Lucy, Steve and Vanessa.

We also found the prayers of the group of people who agreed to pray for us as we embarked on this journey invaluable. We knew we needed specific prayer covering for this project and we felt held by you all, particularly as we walked through some exceedingly painful times, and were buoyed by your encouragements – thank you so much.

Thank you, too, to those of you who have prayed faithfully for us as a couple for years, including our River Church family. We know your prayers have truly made a difference.

From Claire: Steve, thank you for showing such grace to me over the years, and for agreeing to go on this new adventure of sharing our journey in order to encourage and equip others.

From Steve: Claire, thank you for encouraging me to be honest about our mistakes and to reach deeper into God's grace for our marriage.

Finally, to our Heavenly Father – thank you for bringing us together and for remaining our strong anchor throughout the storms of life. We are so grateful to you for your grace, which we see glimpses of every single day.

Notes

1 Grace Kills Complacency

[1] As the apostle Paul discovered, contentment is something we can and should learn. While imprisoned, we read in Philippians 4, his contentment wasn't something that came by chance. It was developed through worship (v.4) and through contending in prayer (v.6). Paul's whole focus was on Christ. But he also took responsibility for his thought life, focusing on the eternal and bringing every thought in line with the truth (v.8), as well as his actions, demonstrated through simple obedience (v.9). None of this was done in his own strength but 'through him who gives [us the] strength' (v.13). The very presence of Christ was his source of peace and contentment, but it was something he fought for. I recognized that many of the things that helped Paul find contentment had been missing from my life. Much of my journey from complacency towards contentment, therefore, has involved reprioritizing and fighting for these very things.

[2] Claire Musters, *Taking Off the Mask* (Milton Keynes: Authentic Media Ltd, 2017).

2 Grace Covers Me

[1] Claire Musters, *Taking Off the Mask* (Milton Keynes: Authentic Media Ltd, 2017).

2   R.T. Kendall, *Total Forgiveness* (London: Hodder & Stoughton, first published 2001, this edition 2010).

3 Grace Chooses to Trust

1   *Definition of trust* [online]. Oxford University Press (2019). https://www.lexico.com/en/definition/trust# (accessed November 2019).

4 Grace Extends Forgiveness

1   R.T. Kendall, *Total Forgiveness* (London: Hodder & Stoughton, first published 2001, this edition 2010).
2   I explore this in more detail along with Chris Ledger in *Insight into Self-Acceptance* (Farnham: CWR, first published 2016, reprinted 2019).
3   Dan B. Allender and Tremper Longman III, *Bold Love* (Colorado Springs, CO: NavPress, 1992).
4   We are certainly not advocating overlooking behaviour that puts you, or any children you may have, in danger.

5 Grace Seeks to Understand

1   Gary Thomas, *Sacred Marriage* (Grand Rapids, MI: Zondervan, 2000), p.50.
2   Nicky and Sila Lee, *The Marriage Book* (London: Alpha International, 2010).
3   R.T. Kendall, *Your Words Have Power* (London: Hodder & Stoughton, 2006).
4   Zoe is a general grief expert, with a specialized interest in baby and child loss and pregnancy after loss. She is the author of four books, *Saying Goodbye*, *The Baby Loss Guide*, *Beyond Goodbye* and *Pregnancy After Loss*, which help people navigate grief and the pain of loss. For more information see: https://www.zoeadelle.co.uk and https://www.mariposatrust.org.

7 Grace in Times of Conflict

[1] Chris Ledger and Claire Musters, *Insight into Managing Conflict* (Farnham: CWR, 2014), p.37.

8 Grace Takes Responsibility

[1] This is something that Steve and I faced afresh as the Coronavirus pandemic escalated: he was focused on providing live streaming for Sunday services, video link ups for small groups and ensuring everyone was pastorally cared for, while I was on tenterhooks, checking each day whether my mum's funeral was still going to go ahead. We were both so emotionally invested in what we were doing, both run down, and we each struggled to support the other.

[2] Sharon Brown, *Sensible Shoes* (Downers Grove, IL: InterVarsity Press, 2013).

[3] If you would like to find out more about utilizing the Daily Examen in your everyday life, here is a useful starting point: https://www.ignatianspirituality.com/ignatian-prayer/the-examen/.

[4] Jan Johnson, *Invitation to the Jesus Life* (Colorado Spring, CO: NavPress, 2008).

[5] Emma first used this description at https://emmascrivener.net/my-story/ (accessed 19 December 2019).

[6] Glen first discussed this at https://emmascrivener.net/2012/12/love-in-the-darkness/ (accessed 19 December 2019).

10 Grace Champions the Other

[1] You might want to spend some time together looking up these verses and discussing them – and their impact on your life. A simple online search for 'one anothering verses' will bring up a wealth of websites if you would like some help locating them.

2 *Definition of cherish* [online]. Oxford University Press (2020). https://www.lexico.com/en/definition/cherish (accessed 3 March 2020).
3 Gary Thomas, *Cherish* (Grand Rapids, MI: Zondervan, 2017).
4 Please understand we are not advising anyone to put up with behaviour that is abusive – this is about learning to overlook the day-to-day annoyances and not allowing misunderstandings and upset to cause bitterness to grow in an otherwise healthy marriage.

11 Grace for the Unexpected

1 Jerry Sittser, *A Grace Disguised* (Grand Rapids, MI: Zondervan, first published 1995, revised edition 2004).
2 Find out more about their charity at https://www.kintsugihope.com.
3 Patrick Regan, *When Faith Gets Shaken* (Oxford: Monarch Books, 2015).
4 Based on analysis of the June questionnaire for the 'UK Household Longitudinal Survey Coronavirus Study' (University of Essex 2020). To read the report by Harry Benson and Stephen McKay visit https://marriagefoundation.org.uk/research/has-lockdown-strengthened-marriages/ (accessed 17 November 2020).

12 Grace Lasts the Distance

1 If you would be interested in reading Lucy's blog on *The Crown*, you can find it at: https://thehopefilledfamily.com/the-crown-four-marriage-lessons/ (accessed 1 June 2020).
2 https://lessonsfromhome.co/embracing-a-life-of-gratitude-when-marriage-is-not-beautiful/?fbclid=IwAR3Qks45lXHmF4jnQQdhkKJYElqfS1Xorvn-A-eltvBW4Y65mo53_XLcQo4 (accessed 28 November 2019).